MW01196071

JOANNE GODDARD

Fayetteville, Georgia 30214

ISBN-13: 978-1545107492

ISBN-10: 1545107491

All artwork done by Grant Edwards

All editing and formatting done by Stephanie Anderson and Scribez Editorial Services

All scripture quotations, unless otherwise indicated, are taken from the King James Version (Authorized Version). First published in 1611.

Interrupted
TO INTERCEDE

CHALLENGING **YOU** TO EMBRACE THE **DIVINE** DISRUPTIONS IN YOUR **LIFE**

JOANNE**GODDARD**

CONTENTS

ACKNOWLEDGEMENTS

There are several individuals that mean the world to me. They have played a key role in me writing this book. First and foremost, I want to dedicate this book to my Senior Pastors, Apostle Bryan and First Lady Patrice Meadows. Without your inspiration, chances are, this book wouldn't exist. The love you've shown, the sacrifices you've made on my behalf, the wisdom and encouragement you've imparted, and the patience you've displayed has made me a wiser and better person. You stretched me even when I resisted. You recognized the gifts God placed within me and kept believing in me! With great skill you activated those gifts. You created a platform for me and placed a demand on my gifts, calling, and anointing. You literally loved, pushed, and prayed me into purpose. I owe so much of my spiritual growth and development to you. You are my examples of integrity, strength, faithfulness, greatness, and excellence. Thank you for being an amazing spiritual covering for me. I love you so much!

To my spiritual sisters, Prophetess Trena Montgomery, Elder Vanessa Hunter, and Minister Roberta Axson. You prayed with and for me through the ups and downs of my life. What a roller coaster ride it has been! Yet, you stayed on the journey with me. We've cried and laughed together many times. The words of wisdom you guys imparted were priceless. You've been amazing role models of mighty women of God poised in strength, grace, and powerful anointing. To one of my mentors and brother in Christ, Apostle Johnny Baugh, who interceded many times for me. You taught me so much primarily by your life's example and keen discernment. What I gained through those Saturday evening prayer meetings have yet to fully manifest. I'm forever thankful for how God used each of you to deposit what was needed along the way.

Last, but certainly not least, to my two precious children, Timothy and Brittany. Being your mother and having the awesome responsibility of raising you up in the fear of the Lord has caused me to assume my intercessory position perhaps more often than I'd like. When all is said and done, I know it will be worth it. It's my earnest desire that the Lord would raise you up to be men and women of prayer. May the womb of intercession break forth in your lives. I decree and declare that you shall experience God's power, glory, and the supernatural as a result of it. Words are not adequate to sum up how much I value each and every one of you. Thank you for helping me become the woman of God that I am today. I love you all dearly!

- Joanne Goddard

INTRODUCTION

The Purpose of This Book

Has your life ever been interrupted? If you are human, I'm quite sure it has. I liken my life to a roller coaster ride. The ups and downs are way too many to count. I have felt dizzy and nearly wanted to puke every time I was on a bumpy "twister like" ride. In the past, I've experienced sleepless nights, betrayal, divorce, abuse, neglect, sickness, sudden loss, abandonment, being misunderstood, fear, failure, guilt, shame, humiliation, and the list goes on and on. For years I was angry at God. Every chance I got, I argued with Him. I felt greatly justified in putting up balloons, getting the biggest cake with the words WOE IS ME written across it, gave an invitation to sorrow, depression, gloom, discouragement, bitterness, and then danced to the beat of my own pity party. I am thankful that despite and in spite of all that I've gone through, God walked with me every step of the way. He never abandoned me. Neither did He pay much attention to my childish tantrums. Although He didn't cause it, God made sure that the hurt that was allowed in my life would not go to waste and would not be in vain. He would use all of the turbulence for His glory. ***Romans 8:28*** *(NKJV) "And we know that all things work together for good to those who love God, to those who are called according to His purpose."* I had to be purged, broken, and humbled for a greater plan; a divine plan. A.W. Tozer said so eloquently "It is doubtful that God can bless and use a man greatly until he's been hurt deeply."

As I began to mature in my walk and relationship with the Lord, I realized the tests, trials, and hardships were indeed part of the **PROCESS** for a greater **PURPOSE**.

—

2 Corinthians 1: 3 and 4 *(NKJV) says "Blessed be the God and Father of our Lord Jesus Christ, the Father of mercies and God of all comfort, who comforts us in all our tribulation, that we may be able to comfort those who are in any trouble, with the comfort with which we ourselves are comforted by God."* There are many ways by which comfort is released to the Body of Christ. Though not an exhaustive list, people experience comfort through worship songs, meditation, scripture reading, words of encouragement, someone simply being present, offering a listening ear or a shoulder to cry on, loyalty, faithfulness, dependability etc. There remains a powerful way by which comfort is activated on behalf of a place, person, or situation, and that is through **intercession**.

The pain of life produced pressure, which gave way to a breaking in me that keeps my heart tender for the hurt and pain of people, situations, cities, and nations. In my particular case, my life was **INTERRUPTED,** in so many ways and so many times, so I could **INTERCEDE**. You see, it was never about me. God was always thinking about the World. While I was crying and weeping for ME and MY situation (which represents one tiny speck of sand), God was overlooking and weeping for the entire shore (which represents the WORLD). This book was written for every Christian who has ever posed the question "Why me? Why am I going through this situation?" Well, why not you? Did you ever consider that God may be **PREPARING** you? All the heartbreaks, mistakes, stress, disappointments, curveballs, detours, twists, and bumps in the road may very well be sudden **INTERRUPTIONS** leading to your God-given purpose. Scripture says in *Jeremiah 29:11 (NKJV) "For I know the thoughts that I think toward you, says the Lord, thoughts of peace and not of evil, to give you a future and a hope..."*

If you continue to kick, scream, wail, and holler, then you've missed the **TRUTH** or revelation behind the **TURMOIL**. If you yield to the process, God will use the interruption to cause you to be a hand, foot, mouth, or an ear that can touch the world on heaven's behalf. *Ephesians 2:10 (NKJV) "For we are His workmanship, created in Christ Jesus for good works, which God prepared beforehand that we should walk in them."*

This book is comprised of several chapters. In the first section of each chapter, I share a few personal experiences, life's struggles, or sudden interruptions (many times my daily routine, schedule, or sleep was interrupted) that the Lord used to prepare me for ministry. It was through the disruptions that I was broken, molded, purged, fashioned, and my heart made tender. God has graced me with many gifts and assignments for the edification of the Body of Christ. Of all the assignments given to me, I am most passionate and burdened about the task of a Prophetic Intercessor. In the second section of each chapter I offer some powerful intercessory nuggets that you can chew on as you embark on your own intercessory journey.

You may have been called to pastor a church, direct a choir, write worship songs, evangelize to your own family, or serve as a missionary in Ecuador. Regardless of the call, there is usually a divine disruption to propel you to your destiny. If you don't believe me, ask Abraham who was asked to leave his comfort zone to go to a land that God would show him. Go ahead and ask David who was minding his business in the backfields of the wilderness when Samuel sought to anoint a new king for Israel. Feel free to converse with Joseph who experienced pit, slavery, prison, and palace all in one lifetime. Don't stop there! You may want to study the lives of Moses, Esther, Ruth, Jeremiah, Isaiah, Ezekiel, Mary, the twelve disciples, Paul, Jesus Himself, and many others in the Bible whose lives were interrupted.

Their interruptions were never for "me, myself, and I" reasons as some have initially thought, but for ministry to and for others.

First and foremost, it is my earnest prayer that after reading this book, you would no longer ask "Why me Lord?" but rather "Lord what is the purpose behind these disruptions in my life?" Last but not least, for those that feel a burden or calling to intercede, I trust this book will provide you with valuable insights pertaining to intercession. For those currently serving as intercessors in your church, you may find yourself nodding your head as you relate to some of my personal experiences regarding intercession. On the other hand, your own memories of times you were interrupted to intercede may be recalled. Whatever purpose this book serves for you, may it leave you with a sense that "It's not about me. There's a greater purpose behind my pain!" Come join me on this journey of embracing your divine interruptions!

Chapter One:

"WHAT DO YOU MEAN SHE'S NOT MY MOTHER?"

$\mathscr{I}$recall the feelings of disbelief, confusion and betrayal at the tender age of 8 when my dad told me that my stepmother was not my real mom. 'What? What do you mean? I've been calling her mommy. Where was my real mom?' These were the questions swirling in my head. If we've been living a lie did they understand this would change everything for me? This was huge. The real world as I knew it came crashing down. It felt as if someone yanked a rug out from underneath me, and then beat me senselessly over the head with the same rug. Boy was I livid! How could they lie to me all this time? 'Look at her, pretending she's my mother. And my father, who was he really? What imposters!' I thought to myself.

What led up to this confession? Well, we have to back track a bit. I was born in Brooklyn, NY on December 14, 1971. Two years later, my siblings who are fraternal twins, were born on January 3, 1973. According to her death certificate which is currently in my possession, my real mom Jacqueline Raymond-Kebreau died two days after giving birth to the twins. She left behind three infant children. My father who was experiencing utmost distress, needed to get himself together, decided to send my siblings and me to Haiti, to live with my grandparents. Gathering seashells at the beach, living in a decent house, playing with a huge dog, and eating fruits someone picked right off a tree are the extent of my memories during the time I lived with my grandparents.

At some point in time, my grandparents explained that we were being reunited with my father. Next thing I knew, we were back in the states. I was now five years old, my siblings three and a half. We were residing with my dad and my mother (at least we automatically assumed she was mom). No one ever told us differently. For the next three years, I loved and related to my stepmother as my real mother. I called her mommy. One day, although I was too young to remember what it was, something important was being discussed.

My father pulled my siblings and me to the side and disclosed that my stepmother was not my real mother. Sheer devastation took over.

Based on the culture that my family came from, children were not allowed to raise questions. A huge hole sank deep within me. Only about two years later (around age 10) was it finally disclosed to us that my real mom had passed away. No one explained how or why. The hollow place within me became a thousand times bigger than it was before. I secretly resented my stepmother and father. I felt they should have told me from the very start before I embraced this woman as my real mother. I didn't care for the three years of pretense. I wanted my real mother. Why did she pass away? Why did she leave us? What did she look like? What kind of person was she? What would she be doing with us if she were alive? Oh how I missed her! I felt abandoned. To be honest with you there is nothing that anyone could have said that would have consoled me.

It didn't help when my younger sister (my stepmom and dad's biological daughter) was born. I noticed how my stepmother treated her differently from how she treated me and my siblings. She was more patient with her. My youngest sister received the majority of the attention and had many birthday parties. She had more clothes than we did (nicer and more expensive) while the rest of us rotated a few shirts, dresses, and pants. I have to say though that we were always clean, our hair was kept combed, and we were presentable. I don't think my stepmother did it intentionally. People tend to have heartfelt love and a stronger bond with their biological children than with a child they didn't birth.

Fast forward to today, I still call my stepmother mommy, and thanks be to God I have a wonderful relationship with her. I believed she was thrust into a situation where she had to care for three kids that were not her own.

Back then, my stepmother was a young mother herself. She really did the best that she knew how. For me, this painful experience was very real at that time. It changed my life drastically! As a young child, I began to view everyone and everything around me through hazy/blurred lenses. The betrayal, resentment, and all the questions I had left an imprint that affected me for years to come. My relational foundation with those I trusted was now rocky and unstable. I couldn't depend on or trust anyone. I walked around with hurt on my shoulders. I was unsure of myself. In my first year of college, I was already a Christian but was at a low place in my life. I felt alone. I was in despair. One day, I went home, entered my room and was determined to commit suicide. I had a bottle of pills in my hand.

As I contemplated taking the entire bottle, an inner or outer voice directed me to glance at the Bible that was opened under my pillow. I used to leave my Bible open under the pillow (I guess I was a bit superstitious). Tears filled my eyes. I was depressed, felt abandoned by my biological mother, and by everyone else. With nothing to lose, I pulled the Bible from underneath the pillow. The page of the Bible was opened to *Psalm 27*. Immediately, I looked at a verse I had never read or knew existed. It was *Psalm 27:10* *"When my father and my mother forsake me, then the Lord will take care of me."* At that very moment God let me know that He was there. No matter who I felt had abandoned me, He was a present help and would take care of me. I wept and wept and wept. It was such a divine intervention and revelation. I wish I could tell you that all was well after that. By no means! The challenges of life had only begun. By the grace of God, I am alive telling my story.

A few years later, when I turned twenty-five, I wept for two hours straight for my biological mother. The emotions were overwhelming. I missed my mom and wished she was there to see me turn into a grown woman.

13

It was like a purging. I was letting go of years of unforgiveness towards my mom for dying before I got a chance to know her. I was releasing a pain that was buried deep in my soul. I would liken it to a mini deliverance. I still miss my mom and occasionally shed a tear for her when major events take place in my life. But the tears are brief, and no longer prolonged.

Watching the news on television can be very difficult at times. I find myself weeping, my stomach begins to ache, and I begin to intercede automatically when I hear that children are missing, abducted, died of neglect, are orphans, or are abused at the hands of a loved one. Where are their parents? Who has betrayed them? A righteous indignation wells up within me. These are questions that are too close to home. I feel a burden for these children. Children are dear to the heart of God. When children hurt, God hurts. When they cry, God cries. My hearts aches for the children just as God's heart aches. Why do I feel this way you might ask? Burdens from heaven are usually downloaded onto the hard drive of an intercessor. Therefore, it becomes the responsibility of an intercessor to stand before God on behalf of man through prayer (this is the opposite of a prophet who normally goes to man on behalf of God). In the Bible, there were three significant anointings (sometimes referred to as offices). There was the anointing of the King, the Priest, and the Prophet. Our Lord and Savior Jesus Christ occupies every single one of these offices and is Himself the embodiment or essence of all three anointings. Here are a few, confirming scriptural references for you:

Revelation 17:14 *(NKJV) These will make war with the Lamb, and the Lamb will overcome them, for He is Lord of lords and* ***King of kings****; and those who are with Him are called, chosen, and faithful."*

Hebrews 4:14-16 *(NKJV) Seeing then that we have a great* ***High Priest*** *who has passed through the heavens, Jesus the Son of God, let us hold fast our confession. For we do not have a*

High Priest who cannot sympathize with our weaknesses, but was in all points tempted as we are, yet without sin. Let us therefore come boldly to the throne of grace, that we may obtain mercy and find grace to help in time of need.

Matthew 21:11 *(NKJV) So the multitudes said, "This is Jesus, the prophet from Nazareth of Galilee."* And **John 4:19** *The woman said to Him, "Sir, I perceive that You are a **prophet**."*

You will find that true prophets are birthed through the canal of intercession. In order for them to fulfill their assignments, intercession becomes a lifestyle. However, our focus here is not so much on prophets, but the priests. We will deal with Prophetic Intercession in a later chapter. The intercessory functions mostly mirror that of the priest, who throughout scripture, served as a mediator between God and His people. The duties of the priest involved repenting in the stead of the people, offering the sacrifices of the people to God, and inquiring of God on behalf of nations and much more. The priest carried the people and their needs before the Lord. The priest was an intercessor. When intercession is activated, there are some significant things that normally occur:

1. Intercessors usually feel the pain or emotions that God and heaven feels. Intercessors are God's ambassadors. Intercessors are heaven's representatives. It's not about coming before God with a laundry list of your own prayer requests that need to be met. It is praying what is on heaven's agenda. That agenda involves the globe and not one's own selfish desires. It's the *"Your kingdom come, your will be done on earth as it is in heaven (**Matthew 6:10** NKJV)"* type of prayer. Therefore, intercession is about tapping into the spirit realm and sensing the heart and mind of God for the world around us. God's heart is burdened for a lost and dying world. When you tap into God's heart and mind, you get His emotions. Did you know that God has emotions? We know that God is spirit. But yes, He also has feelings.

Through His Holy Spirit, the raw emotions of God are expressed through His people. Various accounts throughout scripture demonstrate that God can be pleased, displeased, grieved, angry etc. God is also compassionate as mentioned in *Matthew 9:36 (NKJV)*, *"But when He saw the multitudes, He was moved with compassion for them, because they were weary and scattered, like sheep having no shepherd."*

It is important to mention that those who are called to be intercessors will experience their hearts being tenderized. They will often feel emotions they didn't sign up for. Intercessors will weep, hurt, laugh, groan, moan, etc. Just like God, their hearts and spirit may be grieved over someone or a situation.

2. Since the intercessor comes on man's behalf and stands in man's stead, they normally take on the burdens that man experiences. Emotions are certainly involved here but this is more than weeping for someone. It's as though you become the individual going through the situation. For example, an intercessor may be praying for someone with heart disease and suddenly find themselves experiencing chest pains. Or they may be interceding for someone with arthritis and may begin to feel pain in their arms or legs. Intercessors can also take on the griefs that others feel. Intercessors may find themselves feeling sorrowful when praying for a child who is sad, due to being abandoned. Believe it or not, this often comes with the territory. Remember that scripture says that Jesus who knew no sin became sin for us *(2 Corinthians 5:21)*. Jesus was the sacrificial lamb. He was our scapegoat. The World English dictionary defines scapegoat as **a person or group made to bear the blame for others or to suffer in their place.** *Isaiah 53:3 (NKJV)* says *He is despised and rejected by men, A Man of sorrows and acquainted with grief. And we hid, as it were, our faces from Him; He was despised, and we*

did not esteem Him. Jesus took on what we were supposed to bear. And Jesus Himself is an Intercessor. **Hebrews 7:25** *(NKJV) Therefore He is also able to save to the uttermost those who come to God through Him, since He always lives to make intercession for them.* Therefore, through intercession, the burdens of others are carried by Intercessors.

Earlier, I mentioned experiencing a pain in my belly. What was that about? Most intercessors have experienced travail at one point or another. I travail a lot (usually in my private time with the Lord). Everyone's experience may differ but there are some commonalities during a time of travail. Travailing prayer is a manifestation of the grief of the heart of God. It is a deep cry unto God. Usually during travail, most intercessors feel pain in their stomachs. It really does hurt and that is what causes one to cry aloud. The crying out can be accompanied by visible tears. Other times, it is just a cry and hurt from deep within. **Romans 8:26-27** *"Likewise the Spirit also helps in our weaknesses. For we do not know what we should pray for as we ought, but the Spirit Himself makes intercession for us with groaning's which cannot be uttered. Now He who searches the hearts knows what the mind of the Spirit is because He makes intercession for the saints according to the will of God."* Travail is likened to labor pains when a mother's body prepares to give birth to a child. We see an example of this from the words of Apostle Paul in **Galatians 4:19**) "My little children, of whom I travail in birth again until Christ be formed in you". In **Jeremiah 30:5-6**, we find another account of travailing: *"For thus saith the Lord; We have heard a voice of trembling, of fear, and not of peace. Ask ye now, and see whether a man doth travail with child? wherefore do I see every man with his hands on his loins, as a woman in travail, and all faces are turned into paleness?"* Just like in childbirth, one pushes until the newborn makes an entrance into the world. Travail is for the purpose of birthing spiritual sons, birthing something and bringing it into manifestation in the earth realm, destroying bonds, yokes, chains, etc. so that people can experience spiritual freedom. When intercessors are travailing, they are burdened. They must continue to groan, moan, and intercede until they feel a release. Your body just senses when the burden has lifted. All your inner muscles begin to relax and the tension is eased. Sometimes, the burden lifts for just that moment but resumes when battering ram prayers are necessary (I will explain this later on in the book). I am a mother and I have experienced labor pains first hand. I could not imagine pushing with no end in sight. At some point in time, the pressure applied to the uterus is an indication that it's time to give birth. Every woman who has been blessed to give birth naturally can testify that prior to labor, they were in great anticipation to behold their precious, little bundle. As it is in the natural, so it is in the spiritual. There is a reward, goal, aim, objective behind intercession. Thank heavens that travailing does not endure forever. If it did, it wouldn't be scriptural. *Psalm 126:5-6* says *"Those who sow in tears shall reap in joy. He who continually goes forth weeping bearing seed for sowing, shall doubtless come again with rejoicing, bearing his sheaves with him."* *Ecclesiastes 3:4* states, *"A time to weep, and a time to laugh; a time to mourn, and a time to dance"*.

If the truth be told, every child longs for a mother, and the majority of women desire to bear a child. But what happens when you can't seem to deliver a child either in the natural or in the spirit? Have you ever reached a place in your life where you felt boxed in? Ever felt restricted? You just needed more room. You just needed an opportunity. Something was brewing and crying deep down in your soul for what God had next for you. You know that you can no longer stay on the level that you are on. Even though sometimes we feel stuck or in between places, there is no holding pattern in God. You have decided you won't go back, but where you are is just not it for you either. You just want MORE, and rightfully so, because the Bible says the Lord will take us from glory to glory, faith to faith, strength to strength, so there is more to be obtained.

In *1 Samuel 1:1-20* we come across a woman by the name of Hannah that knew first- hand what it was to be empty and barren. Hannah was married to a wealthy man by the name of Elkanah. From the passage we read that Elkanah had two wives Peninnah who had children and Hannah who had none. It's probable that Elkanah married Hannah first, but because she had no children he married Peninnah to give him many children. However, he loved Hannah more than Peninnah. So much so, that gave her a double portion of meat and all that he had. I think it was not only because he favored Hannah but because she didn't have any children. Elkanah was probably trying to get Hannah's mind off of her barrenness but Hannah was still miserable. Back in those days to be childless was considered a curse and a disgrace. It was a reason to feel ashamed. Was there something wrong that God had closed up Hannah's womb? That's what people believed. Imagine the speculation as to why. Even today in India women who have no children are pointed out in the street, laughed at, and talked about. It's a stigma. Therefore, Hannah felt like a failure as a woman and as a wife. To make matters worse, Hannah had to endure the teasing and taunting from Peninnah, the enemy's show off.

Elkanah would say to Hannah "Why are you weeping? Why are you not eating? Why are you depressed? Am I not enough? Am I not better to you than ten sons?" In the eyes of others, it appears we have it all. But you can have so much yet possess so little. Very few people know what you really need or desire except you and God. Hannah was not satisfied. She was depressed, despondent, and downcast. The house wasn't enough. The car wasn't enough. Hannah wanted MORE! She was HUNGRY! There was something in particular that she wanted and she would not rest until she had it. Hannah realized what she needed was not OUTSIDE of her but WITHIN. She had to birth destiny. She had to push something out. Her own dreams had to be fulfilled.

Hannah reached the place where she said "Enough is Enough!" She decided she was no longer going to be bitter but better. Hannah knew she could no longer stay in the position that she was in. She became desperate. She was hungry and thirsty for more. Hannah pressed her way into the tabernacle but this time with a different attitude. Now, when women entered the temple to worship, they were expected to worship reverently. Hannah was in anguish and poured out her soul before the Lord. Although no words came out, her lips were moving. She was so beside herself that it appeared to Eli (the priest) that she was drunk. But she wasn't drunk, she was desperate. Desperate times call for desperate measures! Hannah went into intercessory mode.

I'm quite certain this was not the first time Hannah prayed to God. Before, she might have wanted a child just for herself, for her own selfish reasons. Perhaps she wanted to prove to Peninnah that she too could have children. But in verses 9-18, something changed. Hannah said, "Lord, I've been asking you for a child for all the wrong reasons. Concerning this thing that I desire, what is your will and your purpose for it?" She promised God that if he allowed her to bear a child, she would give that child back to Him. God owns cattle on a thousand hills. The earth is the Lord's and the fullness thereof. Scripture says that God's arms are not short that they cannot save or deliver. His ears are not deaf that He cannot hear. Understand that God always has the means and the methods. He's just waiting for us to have the right motives. We can desire the right things but for the wrong reasons.

In verse 20 of *1 Samuel 1*, Hannah bore a son and named him Samuel. Hannah kept her son until he was weaned, probably at about 3 years old. What happened to Samuel? He was turned over to Eli the priest to be mentored by him. He stayed and ministered before the Lord under Eli. God called Samuel and he became a prophet to all Israel. Hannah's barrenness was turned into fruitfulness. The Lord continued to be gracious to Hannah. She conceived and gave birth to three sons and two daughters. What would have happened if Hannah settled? What if she never yearned for that child? I challenge you like Hannah to hunger, thirst, and passionately pursue the next level. Intercession is a key that opens wombs, shatters glass ceilings, and breaks heaven open for personal needs, families, cities, regions, nations. BUT our aim in intercession must all be for God's glory!

Isaiah 54:1-3

New King James Version (NKJV)

"Sing, O barren, You who have not borne!
Break forth into singing, and cry aloud,
You who have not labored with child!
For more are the children of the desolate
Than the children of the married woman," says the LORD.
2 "Enlarge the place of your tent,
And let them stretch out the curtains of your dwellings;
Do not spare;
Lengthen your cords,
And strengthen your stakes.
3 For you shall expand to the right and to the left,
And your descendants will inherit the nations,
And make the desolate cities inhabited.

Many of you have correctly read your pregnancy test and can confidently proclaim that you have a seed in your womb. Some of you have been impregnated by a new relationship. Some of you are carrying an astronomical/innovative idea. Many of you are expecting a new business or ministry. Perhaps your church is carrying something significant for souls, for your region. Suffice to say it is not enough to be pregnant. As it is in the natural, so it is in the spirit. There are stages/trimesters of pregnancy. Every stage must be properly discerned, developed, and guarded to avoid any spiritual abortions, premature births, or stillbirths. We know that whenever God desires to accomplish something in the earth realm, He uses His people. Therefore, the Lord in His infinite wisdom has given the Body of Christ one of the greatest gifts known to man to protect every divine pregnancy, and that is the gift of midwives. As described above, an intercessor can be likened to a woman giving birth. But flip the same coin and an intercessor also assumes the role of a midwife.

What were the functions of a Midwife?

- Midwives were trained, skilled professionals that came alongside a pregnant woman during prenatal care, labor, delivery, and after the birth of the baby.
- When a woman finds out she is pregnant, there is level of excitement, but also fear because she's never been that way before (especially if it is her first pregnancy). Even if it isn't her first pregnancy, every pregnancy is different so you just never know what to expect and nervousness tends to kick in.
- So first and foremost upon the announcement of the pregnancy, the midwife was a cheerleader. She would say things such as "I'm proud of you." "I'm so happy you are carrying that baby." "All is going to be well." "I know you've never raised a child before but you will

learn and will be an excellent mother." It is absolutely imperative that we have the right people in our circle. Not gossipers, naysayers, assassinators, jealous folk etc. You need a midwife whose tongue is anointed and whose heart is pure.

- Midwives had to be trusted by God and the mother had to trust you. Can you be trusted to handle someone's pregnancy, labor, and delivery?
- Throughout the pregnancy, the midwife would advise the expectant mother to get adequate rest, proper nutrition, wear appropriate clothing, encourage her to keep up with her doctor's visits, and track the growth of the baby in utero.
- During labor, the midwives would monitor the frequency of the contractions, hold the hand of the mother, release encouraging words, let her know they were there, stroke her head, massage her back or belly to keep her as comfortable as possible.

  - Did you write that book yet? How is the business coming along? Your mom is in the hospital? Well, I'm coming to the hospital to sit and pray with you. You're starting a church? Great! I'm going to sow $300 into that building project.

- During delivery, the midwife would coach the woman on when and how to breathe especially during contractions, when to push (I see the head crowning). She helped deliver the baby and washed the baby after the birth.
- After delivery, midwives helped restore the mother's strength as labor and delivery is very draining. The

---

midwife served as a role model for the new mother, teaching her the specifics of how to change diapers, when to feed the baby etc., and would actually help the mother to take care of the baby until the mother was able to do so on her own.

Spiritual midwives are skilled in prayer because nothing happens unless and until we pray. Pease understand that anything we have received outside of the field of prayer is illegal and up for grabs by the kingdom of darkness. You might say, "I didn't pray for this business, I didn't pray for this house, yet the Lord blessed me anyhow." Well you could be reaping from the prayers of midwives such as your momma, grandmother, or the church sister that picked you up in the spirit. Do you have any idea how often your pastor prays for you? Some of the best midwives God has afforded us are pastors and fathers. They will train you, guide you, and coach you to squeeze out all the anointing, pull out all of your gifts, and push you to bring out all of your God given potential. They are guardians over your destiny. This is why you need a spiritual covering.

An example of a biblical midwife that you can study on your own time is Moses from the book of Exodus. He was raised or cared for by midwives (Shifra pseudonym for Jochebed and Puah another name for Miriam). Later on, Moses himself turns around and becomes a midwife to deliver the children of Israel from Egypt. I charge you to engage in intercessory prayer and become a midwife for a person, city, region, or a nation's deliverance.

Chapter Two:

"DON'T TOUCH ME!"

For a great part of my life, I struggled with trusting people. God has truly brought me a mighty long way and has done a tremendous work. I now allow myself to be vulnerable and can open up my heart more easily. But to remain honest with myself and with you, I am still very cautious with specific individuals and in certain situations. Can I just keep it real for a moment here? With the suicide rate among pastors and church leaders increasing, there's no sense in pretending. Many Christians walk into church buildings and are masters at pretentious ways. They smile outwardly, but are hurting deep within. However, they are not to bear the burden of the blame. The Christian culture has trained us to wear masks as if all is well, and it very well could be, but if truth be told, there is an area or many areas in our lives where we are all still under construction.

Now, I am not advocating living in misery or brokenness because that is NOT the will of God. We are to live in peace and not in pieces. Healing has to take place at some point in time. For the Body of Christ and for the sake of God's glory, I pray wholeness takes place sooner than later. For some of us, healing can be instantaneous. For others, it is a process that has to be worked out, like an onion whose layer is peeled back one layer of skin at a time. Yet, all of us have a thorn in the flesh that we bear. There are real issues that we deal with on a daily basis. We strive for perfection and maturity in Christ but the only perfect one is Christ himself. So yes, it often takes a minute for my wall to come down, even as a Christian. With the exception of a few individuals that I trust my life with, others close to me know that what I just stated is not an exaggeration. I am so grateful for my spiritual family who exercised extreme patience with me as they fought to demolish my gigantic barricade.

There is not one isolated incident that I can pinpoint as the cause of this mistrust. Rather, there were many contributing factors and experiences that I have endured. One major, life changing situation, was being called into a room on several occasions, by a trusted and older family member. When he asked me to come to him, I was obedient. It was ingrained in us from an early age that you show respect to your elders. Whatever they asked you to do, you obeyed. In my culture, there was a reverential fear toward adults. Children would not dare talk back to an adult or dare question any directives given. Respect was respect and a child stayed in a child's place (you all know what I'm talking about). The dilemma that presented itself with that cultural norm was that I was not taught what directives to obey nor what instructions to disobey. It was simply OBEY at all costs. Looking back, boy did it cost me! There's an old saying, "What you don't know won't hurt you!" In this particular case, that statement is a lie from the pit of hell. Ignorance is not bliss. I paid a substantial price by simply not understanding.

Whenever my stepmother or father was away from the home, this elderly family member was in charge to look after us. He would look for an opportune time when my siblings were distracted and playing. He would call me into the room and then, darkness fell and light was incarcerated. Just like a mannequin, I froze in a particular position. He touched me. He fondled me. He kissed me and asked me to kiss back. I didn't understand what all this meant. Deep down inside, I felt this was wrong. I was extremely uncomfortable. I was eight years old. It continued for at least three years when this family member visited us while on vacation. I was never physically penetrated. However, the defilement of the touching, fondling, kissing, the smell of his body, the pretense that he cared about me and the betrayal was a major violation.

How dare you touch me! Where was the revelation that I was God's prized possession? Revelation lied dormant while blindness was wide awake. Does not the Word declare that I am the apple of God's eye? Yet, you dishonored the Lord by poking at His eyeball. You hugged me so innocently in front of our family members, yet behind their backs, you transformed into a vulture, seeking whom you might destroy. I was only eight years old! Didn't he understand that I was just an innocent child? He disobeyed kingdom protocol that says, "Touch not my anointed and do my prophet no harm!" Psalm 139:14 says that I was fearfully and wonderfully made. But for years, I lived only in FEAR of my very existence. I didn't want anyone close to me, I didn't want anyone touching me. It wasn't just a physical touch that I became fearful of, more so, it was an emotional touch that petrified me. For the longest time, I refused to connect with others on an emotional and relational level. As a result, I wined, dined, and dated fear. But thanks be to God who has not given me a spirit of fear, but of power, and of love, and of a sound mind. Tears of joy are welling up in my eyes right now because for me to be this transparent and release this painful time in my life is a miracle in and of itself.

Now about the family member who violated me, he passed away years ago. I was able to forgive and release him to God even before his passing. By God's grace, the progress has been and continues to be amazing. I claim total deliverance, freedom, and wholeness daily. I choose to be better and not bitter. I am not a victim but a victor. I have made a conscious decision to trust people again. While the molestation was not my fault, it was still my fight. I didn't have a choice in what happened in my past, but I sure have a choice in what transpires in my future. Devil you thought you won but God sure gave you a black eye. You definitely messed with the wrong one. I am triumphant in Christ!

One evening, I received a phone call from a total stranger. A friend of mine gave her my number and recommended that she call me. The woman on the other end of the line was hysterical and upset. Her young daughter had been acting out at school (talking back to the teacher, hitting other students, saying inappropriate things for her age, and just causing havoc in her classroom). This was now her third school. The woman was afraid this school would also expel her child due to misbehavior. The mother was overwhelmed and at her wits end. She asked me to please pray. My heart went out to her. I immediately began bombarding heaven on her behalf and on the behalf of her young daughter. I started weeping as if it was my own daughter who was going through this. I prayed for God to intervene and for Him to get a hold of this child so that this situation could be turned around. This girl was barely seven years old. So here I am pushing in prayer and pushing in prayer when suddenly, my prayer begins to divinely shift. Holy Spirit rose up within me and with authority I began to say, "Satan, get your filthy hands off…". I said this over and over again. Then, I recall pausing for a minute as if I was listening for instructions. I sensed someone telling me to be quiet and listen. As I listened, I received the download that was needed for this situation.

Then, it all became crystal clear. I told the woman that the reason her daughter was acting out is because someone had molested her. What in the world just happened? How could these words come out of my mouth? I didn't know this lady? But I said what I said with a confidence and surety. There was not a shadow of doubt in my mind. The woman began to weep uncontrollably. She then proceeded to tell me that she had in fact woken up in the middle of the night, looking for her husband, only to find him in her daughter's bedroom.

She confessed that her daughter told her "Mommy, daddy kisses me like he kisses you." Her daughter also pointed to her private part one day and said "Daddy touched me there." The woman was very forthcoming about what she witnessed and heard. She admitted being in denial because after all it was her husband and the girl was the daughter they bore together.

At that point I was overwhelmed but had to compose myself. I immediately got an upset stomach (I literally felt like puking). I almost wish I didn't possess this new found knowledge. It was too much to bear. I took a deep breath and asked her to see her pastor regarding this. It was not my place to counsel. I began to intercede again but this time my prayer was different and very specific. I petitioned that God would give the mother wisdom concerning this situation. I prayed that the decision would be what was ultimately in the best interest of the child. I declared healing for the child. I interceded for the salvation of the father. I pleaded for the mother's strength. I interceded according to revelation. In addition, I wept for this young girl because I know what it's like to be molested. A heart of compassion was necessary. While hell releases inappropriate touches via the fingers of molesters and pedophiles, heaven can touch your life via the technology of intercession.

Please understand that as an intercessor, it is not a requirement that you experience prison, molestation, abandonment, abuse, isolation etc. in order to be moved with compassion or to pray effectively. However, a special grace and anointing is released to break through in prayer for others when you can empathize with them. No one can adequately explain a homeless man's plight like someone who has been homeless themselves. Having walked in the moccasins of another, you truly intercede on another level.

That is why scripture admonishes us that with the same comfort we have received from God, we are now to comfort others *(2 Corinthians 1:3-4)*. Jesus who is God took the form of a man. He was acquainted with our griefs. Today, He is our great intercessor. He intercedes from a place He knows all too well. Remember in chapter one I quoted Apostle Bryan Meadows as saying "Intercession is the strategic pulling down of heaven into the earth realm." The key word to note is strategic. Intercessors must be very strategic when they pray. If not, they will pray amiss. It is imperative that intercessors become sharpshooters with their prayers. Scripture warns us never to lean on our own understanding *(Proverbs 3:5)*. Intercessors need keen discernment to guide them as they intercede. You may ask how in the world I knew that the young girl was being molested by her father. This was revealed to me by a word of knowledge. Word of Knowledge is a gift of the Holy Spirit as outlined in *1 Corinthians 12:8-10 (NKJV)* *"for to one is given the word of wisdom through the Spirit, to another the word of knowledge through the same Spirit, to another faith by the same Spirit, to another gifts of healings by the same Spirit, to another the working of miracles, to another prophecy, to another discerning of spirits, to another different kinds of tongues, to another the interpretation of tongues."*

There are a total of 9 manifestation gifts given by the Holy Spirit. Three are speaking/vocal gifts (prophecy, diverse tongues, and interpretation of tongues). Three are revelation gifts (discerning of spirits, word of wisdom, and word of knowledge). The remaining three are power gifts (gift of healing, working of miracles, and the gift of faith). Christians and Intercessors are not limited to just one gift or one grouping of gifts (such as power gifts). However, it is important to point out that you will find many intercessors operating in one or more of the revelation gifts all at the same time or at different times. Why is this you ask?

How can one pray specifically without revelation? ***Proverbs 25:2*** *(NKJV)* says *"It is the glory of God to conceal a matter, But the glory of kings is to search out a matter."*

God has made us spiritual kings and priests. By our yielding to the Holy Spirit, we can search out a matter and obtain the revelation that we need when maneuvering in the spirit realm (because prayer/intercession is a spiritual activity). Mysteries can be revealed and made known to intercessors. Again, intercessors move heavily in the revelation gifts. Below there is some brief information that will help you better understand the three revelation gifts mentioned above:

Word of Knowledge

- The Greek phrase logos gnosis means word of knowledge, which can literally be "a message"

- Matthew Henry defines word of knowledge as: the knowledge of mysteries

- A message that provides needed information to the Body of Christ

- The message may provide direction

- The message may provide information or it may provide warnings

- The supernatural ability to apply knowledge the proper way

- This word can come in the form of a dream, revelation, a vision or audible voice

- A small portion of God's total knowledge supernaturally imparted by the Holy Spirit

- A revelation of things past or present; never future

- The speaking forth of that knowledge to others

- God given insight and understanding of truth

- Similar to the gift of prophecy, differs in that the word of knowledge does not foretell futuristic facts

- The gift of the word of knowledge works interactively with the other two revelation gifts: wisdom and discernment

Word of Wisdom

There are three types of wisdom:

- The wisdom of God *(1 Corinthians 2:6-7)*

- The wisdom of the world *(1 Corinthians 2:6)*

- The wisdom of man *(Ecclesiastes 1:16-18)*

The gift of the word of wisdom is the application of knowledge that God gives you *(1 Corinthians 2:6-7)*. This type of wisdom is a gift which cannot be gained through study or experience and should by no means try to replace them. The gift of the word of wisdom is seeing life from God's perspective. As a Christian exercises this gift, he begins to develop a fear of the Lord. This is the *"beginning of wisdom"* according to *Proverbs 1:7*.

The gift of the word of wisdom is also the revealing of prophetic futures; it is speaking hidden truths of what is not known. It is a supernatural perspective to ascertain the divine means for accomplishing God's will in a given situation, and is a divinely given power to apply spiritual intuition in problem solving.

Furthermore, this gift involves having a sense of divine direction, being led by the Holy Spirit to act appropriately in a given set of circumstances, and rightly applying knowledge.

The gift of wisdom is the wisdom of God. It is the supernatural impartation of facts; it is not natural. You can't earn it. It is received from God through prayer *(Ephesians 1:17)*.

The gift of the word of wisdom works interactively with the other two revelation gifts: knowledge and discernment.

Discerning of Spirits

- The supernatural power given by the Holy Spirit to perceive the source of a spiritual manifestation and determine its origin
- It is not about finding fault in others, nor is it suspicion or criticism
- Origin of Spiritual Manifestations: From God *Acts 10:30-35*, From Satan *Acts 16:16-18*, and From Man *Acts 8:18-23*
- How to test a Spirit? Observe what a person does, Be a fruit inspector *(Matthew 7:15-20)*, observe whether or not a person exalts Christ as The Son of God, Lord, and Savior, Listen to what a person says, Does their confession agree with the truth of God's word? *(1 John 4:1-3)*

34

- Is applied heavily during Deliverance Ministry and while operating in a prophetic ministry

Always ask God for revelation and insight into a situation before you pray. Scripture warns that we are never to lean on our own understanding. In all our ways we are encouraged to acknowledge God and He shall direct us *(Proverbs 3: 5, 6)*. By doing this, it will prevent us from praying amiss, rather you will pray in alignment with God's will for the individual or circumstance. For example: Brother Nathan may have been laid off of his job and he requests that you pray and agree that he gets another job immediately. On the surface, that sounds like a noble request. What you may not be aware of is that Nathan's previous job consumed his time and served as a distraction from his walk with God. Nathan allowed his job to become an idol. He began to worship mammon rather than the Lord. However, God still has great plans for him. Nathan's release from his job may have been permitted by God in order to bring Nathan back into right standing with the Lord. This may be exactly what Nathan needs to break him, humble him, and cause him to sense his need for God once again.

Now that you are equipped with this knowledge, your prayer for Nathan will probably mirror the following: *"Lord, I bring Nathan before you. Despite his job loss, may you continue to prove yourself faithful to him by supplying all of his needs. During this challenging time, give him revelation that a job is a resource but you are his source. Allow Nathan to reflect and locate himself spiritually. Let him sense his need of you, repent, and get back into right standing with you. I trust that when the timing is right, you will provide my brother with another financial opportunity."* Chances are, the next time Nathan is gainfully employed, he will be a bit more careful not to allow money to become his God.

The revelation gifts are at the disposal of Christians. A gift is a gift and it is given. If you don't possess one or any of the revelation gifts, you can ask God who gives liberally. Sometimes, we witness clustering especially when it comes to the revelation gifts. What I mean by this is that when you've been endowed with one, the operation of the other two begin to manifest. Through the revelation gifts, one can pray pinpoint prayers for people and situations. Why pray according to your own understanding? Why drive a vehicle only to wind up at a dead end? Who has the time to pray aimless? "Not I" said the Evangelist, "Not I" said the Apostle, and "Not I" said the Pastor. There is nothing better than applying the knowledge, wisdom, and discernment of God. These gifts are powerful arsenals in the sphere of intercession and can enable an intercessor to pray specifically and effectively.

Chapter Three:

"SERIOUSLY! YOU LOVE ME?"

$\mathcal{I}$attended Abraham Lincoln High School in Brooklyn, New York from 1985-1989. It was there, in the ninth grade that I met a girl by the name of Nina. Of all the students that I came across, something was definitely different about Nina. She was extremely kind, soft-spoken, and full of joy. Nina was always smiling and gave an encouraging word to everyone that crossed her path. I never witnessed her cursing, gossiping, getting caught up in drama, or engaging in any fights. Nina was by no means popular. As a matter of fact, she was on the opposite end of that spectrum. However, that didn't seem to bother Nina. Everywhere Nina went, she walked with a boldness and confidence as if she owned Abraham Lincoln High School.

From the moment that Nina befriended me, she'd always discuss the Lord. Nina pointed out that tomorrow was not promised to anyone. She made it a habit of posing questions that I didn't have answers to; questions such as, "Where would you go if you died today, heaven or hell?" "Do you know that hell is real? Have you ever given your life to Jesus?" "Are you in right relationship with God?" Almost on a daily basis, Nina expressed that she was praying for me to be saved. I often smiled back at Nina, but in my head I was like "Get saved from what? There's nothing wrong with me!" Surely the devil is a liar and the truth is not in him. I was deceived thinking I didn't need any help. For the first couple of months in high school, I admit, I had my mind on other things and other things to occupy my time with. I paid very little attention to anything that Nina said to me. Her words would go in one ear and out the other. Then, something shifted. I began to focus on Nina's walk. It was no longer what she said. This girl stood out and stood out in a positive way. I admired her difference. Her kindness and joy sparked something within me. Her walk (lifestyle/character) placed a demand on me to pay attention to her talk (words).

Remember I said earlier that I used to tune Nina out? Well in March of 1986, I could tune her out no longer. Our school was a long way off from the train station that we rode home. The walk to the station and ride home was about forty-five minutes. One afternoon, as we walked to catch the Q train, Nina began to explain that we've all sinned against God. She explained how sin separated us from God but that God had provided a way for us to be in right standing with Him again. That way was Jesus Christ. Nina went on to share all that Jesus did (how He left heaven, came to earth, died on the cross, was buried, and rose again) just for me. I asked Nina "Why would Jesus go through all of that." She said it was because He loves me. "Seriously! He loves me?" I exclaimed. "Yes," she answered.

What an amazing thought: someone loves me. Wow! That was mind boggling but certainly peaked my interest to hear more. Nina thoroughly covered the plan of salvation. Nina said all I needed to do was verbally confess the following to God: admit that I was a sinner, state that I believed that Jesus died, was buried and rose for me, then ask Jesus to come into my heart and life and save me. Nina said I could say this confession wherever and whenever I wanted. I recall my heart was just racing while I sat on the Q train. I couldn't wait to get home. Looking back in retrospect, I could have made that confession right there on the train. But understanding how I was wired at the time, I felt I needed to do this privately. When I reached home, I quickly went into my room and closed the door. I knelt down beside my bed, and on Friday, March 14, 1986, at the age of 14, I confessed Jesus and gave my heart to the Lord. When I accepted the Lord as my savior, I saw with my spiritual eyes, a dove enter into the room, and it laid on me as if someone had covered me with a blanket. At the time, I didn't have a clue what that meant. I knew for a fact that I was not hallucinating, and it was not until years later, as I matured as a Christian, that I found out that we are sealed with the Holy Spirit once we are saved.

Throughout scripture, doves are often a representation of the Holy Spirit.

I was so elated about getting saved! I couldn't wait to share the good news with Nina. Nina was ecstatic! She was truly happy for me and we were able to have real discussions about Jesus and being Christian. Now, I wanted the whole world to be saved. With boldness, I began to share Jesus with everyone I ran into. About a year after I got saved, I lost my cool and got into a heated argument with one of my cousins. The incident was so upsetting that I thought I had lost my salvation. That evening, I entered into my room and knelt down by my bedside. In the room, I had a small radio that was always tuned to a gospel station called WWRL.

When I entered the room, the volume on the station was very low. I could barely hear it. I got on my knees and began weeping. I asked God to forgive me and kept asking Him if I was still saved. Suddenly, I was startled by what I heard. The radio station was loud and it was playing this song that said "I'm saved, I'm not gonna die in pain. Through and through I've been made brand new. All my sins are taken away. I'm saved!" I looked around, there was no one in the room. Who turned up the volume? To think of all the gospel songs that could be playing at that very moment, it was a song that answered the question I had about whether I was still saved or not. I was dead wrong! Someone was in the room with me. It was the Lord Jesus Himself. He did all that to let me know that He Loves Me. Seriously! ***John 3:16*** *(NKJV) For God so loved the world that He gave His only begotten Son, that whoever believes in Him should not perish but have everlasting life.*

Whenever I think about my salvation experience, I think of two individuals, Jesus and Nina. I thank God for saving me. He has transformed my life in ways that words cannot merely express. Yet, He had to use a willing and yielded vessel by the name of Nina. You see, I might not be a Christian today if Nina

——

40

did not tell me about Jesus and the plan of salvation. ***Romans 10:14, 15*** *(NKJV) How then shall they call on Him in whom they have not believed? And how shall they believe in Him of whom they have not heard? And how shall they hear without a preacher? And how shall they preach unless they are sent? As it is written: "How beautiful are the feet of those who preach the gospel of peace, Who bring glad tidings of good things!"* Nina did what every Christian is mandated to do and that is to share the gospel with a lost and dying world. As you read this, ask yourself "Who have I witnessed to lately? Does my life match what I say about Christianity and Jesus (is it just talk, or talk and walk)?

So often times, we praise the Billy Grahams, T.D. Jakes of Christendom, and rightfully so. Through their lives and ministry, the lives of countless people have been touched and transformed. They have been called, anointed, and gifted by God to serve the Lord in their generation. And they've done that well. Yet, we rarely ever give thought to who witnessed to Billy Graham or who witnessed to Bishop T.D. Jakes and who in turn witnessed to those individuals. What a crown that awaits these individuals in heaven. I am forever grateful to Nina. I met her at the age of 13 and to this day I've managed to keep in contact with her and we make sure that we touch base several times throughout the year.

You may ask, what does the above story have to do with intercession? It has everything to do with intercession. Nina didn't just witness to me but she prayed and stood in the gap for me. When God interrupts your life to intercede, it is not to waste your time. There is a divine purpose.

God accomplishes a plethora of things through intercession. When we intercede, families are healed, finances are released, dreams and visions are unlocked, doors are open or closed, witty ideas and inventions are given, cities are restored, the sphere of government is influenced for God's glory, sickness and disease are bound, and the list goes on and on. Since it's so powerful, let's pause for a moment and take a closer look at the WHO, WHAT, WHY, WHEN, HOW, and WHERE as it pertains to intercession.

A call for Intercessors

Isaiah 59:16- He saw that there was no man, and wondered that there was no intercessor; therefore his own arm brought salvation for Him; and His own righteousness, it sustained Him.

Isaiah 62:6-7- I have set watchmen on your walls, O Jerusalem; they shall never hold their peace day or night. You who make mention of the Lord, do not keep silent, and give him no rest till He establishes and till He makes Jerusalem a praise in the earth.

What is Intercession?

- Intercession-The strategic pulling down of heaven's will into the earth realm- Apostle Bryan Meadows

- Just like you have the hospitality ministry, the children's ministry, the cleaning ministry etc. at a church, intercession is a prayer ministry.

- To intercede means to serve as a mediator, to intervene as a middle man, and to go in between. An intercessor is one who stands in the gap and goes to God on behalf of man/others. They are watchmen.

- It is engaging in petitionary prayer and can be engaged at any time. At church, home, in your car, your kitchen etc.

- The act of pleading on somebody's behalf- Webster's Dictionary

Who is an Intercessor?

Every believer has the responsibility to be an intercessor at some point in time. However, there are those in the Body of Christ that have a special burden to pray for others. First and foremost, intercessors are themselves, Christians who have confessed Christ as their savior. They have surrendered their lives as vessels for the Lord to use. Intercessors possess God's mind, heart, bear His burdens, and cry His tears. They lend every part of their body to the Lord during intercession. They are usually filled with God's Holy Spirit, with the evidence of speaking in tongues. Lastly, intercessors don't mind their schedules being hijacked by God when it is time to tend to their intercessory assignments.

Why Intercede (The Purpose)

This is not an exhaustive list but here are a few reasons why intercession is needed:

- Manifest Blessings *(Numbers 6:23-27)*

- To see hearts repent and draw near to the Lord *(Romans 10:1-4)*

- To release healing *(James 5:14-16)*; To heal the land *(2 Chronicles 7:14,15)*

- To restore *(Ezekiel 22; Job 48:8-10)*

- To turn away, avert, reverse God's judgment on a people or land *(Numbers 14:11-21)*; *James 2:13*- Mercy triumphs over judgment

- For Deliverance *(1 Samuel 7:5-9)*

—

Intercession is often times initiated by:

- Being awakened suddenly at night- There are many nights where intercessors will not get sufficient sleep

- Visions and dreams

- A face coming to you

- A name you hear/something you hear in the Spirit

- A situation emerging in your mind

- Worship

- Current events/news

- Sudden burdens drop down from heaven

The Power of Intercession

Intercessors exercise executive, legislative, and judicial power. Through their prayers, intercessors have the God given authority to veto, legislate, overthrow, tear down, plant, conquer, subdue, take dominion, shift, change, triumph, possess, destroy, demolish, disrupt, interrupt, deliver, resurrect, restore, inherit, establish and much more.

- *Psalm 2:8*- Ask of Me, and I will give you the nations for your inheritance, and the ends of the earth for your possession.
- *Matthew 7:7, 8*- Ask and it shall be given to you: seek, and you will find. For everyone who asks receives, and he who seeks finds, and to him who knocks it will be opened.
- *James 5:16*- ...The effectual fervent prayer of a righteous man availeth much.

- ***Psalm 8:4-6-*** What is man that You are mindful of him, And the son of man that You visit him? For you have made him a little lower than the angels, And you have crowned him with glory and honor. You have made him to have dominion over the works of Your hands; You have put all things under his feet.

Intercessors Pray Strategic Prayers

There must be strategy for everything we do as Christians and prayer of course is no exception. A method or plan must be carefully thought out and devised as to how we go about intercession. Failure to plan and effectively strategize leaves the kingdom of darkness with the upper hand. There are however two types of prayer strategies: low level and high level.

Low Level Prayer Strategies vs. High Level Strategic Prayer

Low level prayer strategies are the foundational strategies that must be established before entering high level strategic prayer. Just like when a house is being built, you cannot build the roof unless the foundation of the house has been laid. Low level prayer strategies include but are not limited to the following:

1. Plan/schedule specific times for prayer- Prayer that is unplanned or not calculated just won't happen. Praying always on the go is not wise. Remain sensitive because as an intercessor, you will not just pray during scheduled times of prayer but during unplanned/unscheduled times as the need arises.

2. Choose a specific place for prayer- this could be your closet, bathroom, bedroom etc.

3. Set an atmosphere conducive for prayer- You will not be able to pray effectively if the telephone is ringing off the hook or if the TV is on. Find some quiet time. Set the mood for both you and God. You may want to play worship music or self-initiated worship. You may want to light candles. You may want to set a chair for God to come sit next to you. Be creative and do whatever you feel is going to make the setting attractive, comfortable, and pleasing for your prayer experience.

4. Ensure that you have an intimate relationship with God's written Word. There is nothing more powerful than praying scripture and reminding God of His promises.

5. Ensure that you have an intimate relationship with God's Holy Spirit.

6. Make sure you repent of sins of omission and commission and apply the Blood of Jesus. *Psalm 24:3-4* reminds us of the importance of this: Who may ascend into the hill of the Lord? Or who may stand in His holy place? He who has clean hands and a pure heart… There are scripture references such as *Isaiah 59:2* and *Isaiah 11:11* that mentions that the sins of the people causes God to turn a deaf ear to their prayers.

7. Be consistent- In *1 Thessalonians 5:17* the Bible says to pray without ceasing. *Proverbs 18:17* says *"I love those who love me and those who seek me diligently will find me."* Likewise, *Hebrews 11:6* says *God is a rewarder of those who diligently seek Him.*

———

8. Be yourself- When you pray, express yourself through who you really are. Don't try to pray like someone else. God wants to hear from you. Not an imitation of someone else. *In 1 Sam 17:31-39* David refused to wear Saul's armor (verses 38, 39 David had to face Goliath in his own apparels in his own way. Be comfortable in your own skin). Saul's armor represented fear while David's own garments/resources represented faith.

Intercession aims to hit a specific mark. Always remember that the target is not in the natural realm but in the spiritual realm. However, a sharpshooter in intercession (**one with pinpoint accuracy/praying precision prayers**), will inevitably cause there to be a manifestation in the natural realm.

High Level strategic prayer is when you truly enter in and begin to pierce the spirit realm. This is the time and place of access, engagement, warfare, wisdom, revelation, and discernment. Let's briefly look at four aspects of strategic prayer which are warfare, wind, ways, and watches.

1. **Warfare-** Strategic prayer involves heavy warfare and combat therefore, it is NOT for wimps. *Matthew 11:12* reads *"And from the days of John the Baptist until now the kingdom of heaven suffers violence, and the violent take it by force."* Warfare also involves spiritual weapons of mass destruction. That is when the military of God must be deployed. *Ephesians 6:12* says *we do not wrestle against flesh and blood, but against principalities, against powers, against the rulers of the darkness of this age, against spiritual hosts of wickedness in the heavenly places.* In *Genesis Chapter 1* we see a vivid picture of the different spheres of the

military which are three levels of warfare prayer: **Army**- things that creep (deals with land: low level warfare), **Marines & Navy**- things that crawl (deals with the sea: moderate level warfare), and **Airforce** -things that fly (deals with the air: high level warfare). There are detailed revelation given, specific levels of authority granted, and specific things that are accomplished in each sphere. However, all three spheres must be activated and deployed in order for us to be effective in strategic prayer. Please refer to Chapter Five for more on Warfare.

2. **Wind-** *Ephesians 4: 14* *"That we should no longer be children tossed to and fro and carried about with every wind of doctrine, by the trickery of men, in the cunning craftiness of deceitful plotting"*. When we pray we must consider the wind (spirits, atmospheres, moods, motives). Are you praying with bitterness in your heart? What are your motives for praying what you pray? Is there something in the atmosphere that is blocking your prayers? What are the strongholds that first need to be evicted? Sometimes we are aiming for the target, and we are praying consistently, but our prayers still end up falling to the ground because of the blustering winds that are blowing. We must understand forces and events in the spiritual domain that impacts the physical world and vice versa (there are things in the natural domain that impacts the spiritual realm). Jesus had authority to speak to the wind, rebuke it, and command it to be still. We have been given that authority as well.

3. **Ways-** There are various forms of strategic prayer. We must be sensitive to the leading of the Holy Spirit to know which way the Lord is leading us to pray. Strategic Prayer does not always have to be warfare or heavy tongues. However, there are always weapons accessible for us to defeat the enemy and his demonic forces.

   A. Weeping and Wailing Prayer. Tears are a weapon. Every tear has a language and God can interpret your tears.

   B. Brokenness and Repentance- *2 Chronicles 7:14, 15* *"If my people who are called by my name will humble themselves and pray and seek my face and turn from their wicked ways, then I will hear from heaven and will forgive their sin and heal their land." Verse 15 says "Now my eyes will be open and my ears attentive to prayer made in this place."*

   C. Tongues and Groaning (travailing) - *Romans 8:26 Likewise the Spirit also helps in our weaknesses. For we do not know what we should pray for as we ought, but the Spirit Himself makes intercession for us with groaning's which cannot be uttered.*

   D. Decrees and Declarations- *Proverbs 18:21* says *"Death and Life are in the power of the tongue, and those who love it will eat its fruit"*

   E. Thanksgiving

   F. Shouting/marching- In *Joshua Chapter 6* the city of Jericho was given into the hands of the children of Israel when they shouted and marched. Joshua gave specific strategies and instructions in order for them to gain the victory.

G. Worship- In *2 Chronicles 20:20-23* Jehoshaphat sent out worshippers and those who came against Judah destroyed one another.

4. **Watches-** Intercessors can intercede at any time but each intercessor (if they are truly in tune) will notice that they have a specific time whether during the morning or at night whereby they feel most burdened to pray. There are eight prayer watches (which I elaborate on in Chapter Six).

I want to share an acrostic on STRATEGIC intercession. The acrostic below is not my original material. It was information shared on a handout among our intercessory team at a church I attended in the past. I found it to be rather accurate on the necessaries or rules of engaging in intercessory prayer.

- Specific- Strategic Intercession unlocks specific prayers. Our prayers should be exact, precise, and unambiguous. *Psalm 45:1-3*
- Tenacious- our prayers should be obstinate, persistent, insistent, and determined. *Luke 18:1-10*
- Revolutionary- our prayers should be radical, groundbreaking, and world shattering. *Matthew 11:12*
- Authoritative- our prayers should be commanding, confident, imposing, and respected. *Psalm 27:1-4*
- Tactical- our prayers should be deliberate, premeditated, calculated, and intentional. *Hebrews 4:11-13*
- Effective- our prayers should be efficient, valuable, effectual, equipped. *James 5:15-17*
- God-centered- our prayers should glorify God and edify others. *Psalm 19:13-14*
- Inclusive- our prayers should be comprehensive, all-encompassing and complete. *Colossians 4:11-13*

- Conclusive- our prayers should be decisive, ultimate, definite, and irrefutable. *Jeremiah 29:10-12*

Again, we see so much is accomplished and conquered through the power of Strategic Intercession. However, I must emphasize that the objective, basis, intent, purpose, goal, motivation, aim, and big picture of intercession should be the salvation of souls. *Matthew 16:26 (NKJV)* says *"For what profit is it to a man if he gains the whole world, and loses his own soul? Or what will he give in exchange for his soul?"* What good is it if someone is healed of cancer, yet they still end up in hell? What's the point of having an innovative idea that drastically enhances your business, yet you've never had an encounter with Jesus? Relational, emotional, social, physical, and financial advancements are wonderful. But if your soul prospers not, then it is all done in vain. Salvation is the foundation and the running theme throughout the entire Bible. Salvation is on God's heart and mind as outlined in the following scriptures:

2 Corinthians 6:2- *"...Behold now is the acceptable time; behold, now is the day of salvation."*

Acts 13:47- *"For so the Lord has commanded us: I have set you as a light to the Gentiles, that you should be for salvation to the ends of the earth."*

Romans 13:11- *"And do this, knowing the time, that now it is high time to awake out of sleep; for now our salvation is nearer than we first believed."*

Titus 2:11- *"For the grace of God that brings salvation has appeared to all men..."*

Hebrews 2:3- *"...how shall we escape if we neglect so great a salvation, which at the first began to be spoken by the Lord, and was confirmed to us by those who heard Him..."*

---

2 Timothy 2:10- *"Therefore I endure all things for the sake of the elect, that they may also obtain the salvation which is in Christ Jesus with eternal glory."*

Therefore, as an intercessor, whatever the prayer assignment or burden, ultimately you have to hit the bulls-eye and that is to pray for the salvation of individuals, families, communities, cities, states, nations, and the world. Never, ever lose sight of that. In all your spiritual endeavors seek to elevate and highlight ***John 3:16,*** *"God so loved the world that He gave His only begotten Son, that whoever believes in Him should not perish but have everlasting life."*

Chapter Four:

"HOLD UP, WAIT A MINUTE, I'M TRYING TO SLEEP!"

$\mathscr{I}$work every day, raise my kids, pay bills, attend church, am involved in ministry, try to keep up with family and friends, I breathe, sneeze, walk, talk, play, and shop. Yes, like the majority, I lead a busy life. I welcome the time when my head can finally hit the pillow at night. I seize the moment when I can unwind, rest my aching feet, relieve my sore back, and put my racing thoughts on mute. I don't worship sleep but I do look forward to it especially since I survive on not enough sleep. I once heard a preacher say "Sometimes, the most spiritual thing you can do is lay down and get yourself some sleep." I wholeheartedly agree with that statement. I'll shout Hallelujah to that any day!

Psalm 127:2 says God gives His beloved sleep. Of course, I know God loves me tremendously, but if I were to measure His love based on the amount of sleep I usually get, I wouldn't feel beloved by God at all. There are times that I enjoy sleeping through the night. There are other times when my sleep is interrupted in order for me to intercede. It seems as though I am awakened when I am extremely tired. In the flesh, I feel like saying "Hold up, wait a minute here, I'm trying to sleep!" Quickly, I'm reminded by the Holy Spirit that it's not about me, my wants, and my comfort. God's focus is always others.

I remember one night I was awakened so I went into my prayer closet (which happens to be my bathroom). I waited and asked the Lord to show me what He wanted me to intercede for. Immediately, I saw a vision- as though I was looking at a T.V. screen- of a Caucasian male. He was wearing a white t-shirt and a pair of house shorts. He had a beer belly and his hair was disheveled. I saw a Caucasian woman cowering on the ground near him. The man's fist was in a ball like position. He had it raised and was screaming profanities at the woman. He was calling her stupid and pointing out everything that was wrong with her.

His fist remained in mid-air as if he was about to hit her. The woman was definitely afraid. I said "God what are you trying to show me? Do you want me to pray against domestic violence? Do you want me to pray for relationships?" God said "This is happening right now. This is an actual couple. Pray that she gets the strength to leave. She has to exit this volatile relationship."

Another night when my sleep was interrupted, I saw a vision, this time it was a closed vision, of former President Barack Obama. He was standing at a podium giving a speech. I saw three demons dressed in Darth Vader outfits standing side by side directly behind the President of the United States (According to Wikipedia **Darth Vader**, is the central fictional character in the *Star Wars* **universe**. He is an important character in the **expanded universe** of television series, video games, novels, literature and comic books. Originally a **Jedi** prophesied to bring balance to the **Force**, he falls to the **dark side** of **the Force** and serves the evil **Galactic Empire** at the right hand of his **Sith** master, **Darth Sidious**.) I waited to hear what the Lord was saying about this. I was led to pray against the demonic attacks that had been unleashed against President Barack Obama. Following that vision, and clearly portrayed by the media, were months upon months of verbal attacks as well as strategies orchestrated to slander the president's reputation and his work in the White House. Every time I watched something on the news that pertained to the President, I continued to engage in prayer on his behalf.

During a drive home from church, I began to weep uncontrollably. I started to pray in tongues and began to travail (travailing was covered in Chapter One). So much so, that I had to pull the car over so I wouldn't get in an accident. In my spirit, I knew who I was travailing for but didn't know for what. I continued to travail until I felt a release. Then, I drove home. That night, I dreamt about this same individual I was travailing for. In the dream, they were arrested by police and placed in jail. Other than one or two parking tickets, this

—

individual never had any problems with the law. When I woke up the next morning, I disregarded the dream. It seemed like the most unlikely thing. Five months to the day I had the dream, the individual called me collect to inform me that they had been arrested by police and would have to spend the night in jail. I was quickly reminded of the dream five months earlier. I began to pray for this individual. God somehow intervened. This individual spent only one night in jail and was released to go home. When the court date arrived three months later, the end result was that all charges were dropped against him. I honestly believe that even though I disregarded the dream that I had, the tears and travail that went forth on behalf of this individual during that car ride home definitely kept this individual from enduring more heat.

One night, I had an alarming dream. I was sitting in the living room of a friend of mine having a discussion about the Lord. All of a sudden, a black car drives up with tinted windows and begins to spray his house with bullets for a good ten minutes. The vehicle eventually drove off. Because of the dark windows, neither one of us were able to identify who was in the vehicle. We exited the house to assess the damage (which we were sure would be massive). To our surprise, when we walked outside, there was an extremely high fence that encircled the home. But not one broken window, no glass on the concrete, no bullets pierced the door, and everything remained intact. I have never ever dreamt about this male friend before. Therefore, I knew the Lord was trying to send a message and that this dream was meaningful. This was indicative of an oncoming demonic assault. But it also proved that at the end of this attack, all would be well.

I got out of the bed and began to bombard heaven on behalf of my friend. Normally, I don't share my dreams with people that I dream about unless I am led to. I felt a strong urge by Holy Spirit to call him the very next day and share the contents of the dream. I admonished him to pray. My friend listened attentively then thanked me for sharing. A few days later, I left on a ministry trip to London. I was away for two weeks. Upon returning from London, my friend called me and revealed that he had visits with several doctors. They discovered he had cancer. Immediately, the dream came back to our remembrance. My Lord! It was not the house that my friend lives in that the enemy was attacking, but his physical house (his temple). Boy, did his body receive a barrage of bullets via radiation, chemotherapy, and excruciating pain. He's been battling cancer for over two years now. Often, I've had to remind him not to forget how the dream ended. God continues to be a fortress and strong tower for him. Thus far, God has kept him. Many a days and nights I have had to pound heaven's door through intercession not just for my friend but many that battle sickness and disease in their bodies.

These are just a few of the plethora of visions/dreams I've had over the years. Please understand that I share these stories not to make anything sound spooky, weird, or mystical. Christianity is none of the above. Nor do I recount these tales to make myself seem super deep or super spiritual. I promise you I am neither. It is merely to give you insight into the world of an intercessor. The night schedules of intercessors are often disrupted. If you have a normal sleeping pattern and are never awakened at night to intercede for someone or some situation, chances are, you may not have the burden of an intercessor. There are times intercessors will cry out for sleep but sleep will be far away. You don't want to be so bound to slumber that God cannot rely on you to stand in the gap. Many doctors and nurses are often on call for the hospitals that they work for. Well, an intercessor is on call for God.

When Heaven summons, regardless of the time of day or night, it would be wise to report to duty and be found attending your post. Let it never be said of you or of this generation what was expressed in ***Isaiah 59:16***- *He saw that there was no man, and wondered that there was no intercessor; therefore his own arm brought salvation for Him; and His own righteousness, it sustained Him.*

—

In the previous chapter, I mentioned that intercession can be prompted by hearing a name, seeing a face, or visions, and dreams etc. Intercessors tend to have many visions and dreams. Visions are open dreams meaning they are equivalent to seeing a clear picture or watching a movie on a screen, while you are wide awake. Dreams on the other hand are closed visions, which occur while you are sleeping/unconscious. Visions and dreams are vehicles that drives intercession.

We must ensure however that those vehicles are credible. Some visions/dreams appear to be fleeting and may not seem to us to carry a lot of weight. Other visions/dreams are extremely reliable, provide a glimpse into what may be happening in the natural, and are gateways into the spiritual realm. Visions and dreams must be accurately discerned and interpreted. There are many symbols when you are dealing with visions/dreams, therefore, making it almost impossible to take them at face value. Things/people depicted in the visions/dreams are not always what they seem. With that being said, you must never, ever lean on your own understanding. Since I am also a Prophet/Prophetic Intercessor, I would say eight times out of ten, it is immediately revealed to me what a vision or dream is about and the revelation is usually accurate. How do I know? Well, whenever I have a vision or dream, I record it in my spiritual journal. I write down what I sense it is about or the message behind the vision or dream. I also take time to pray about the vision/dream asking the Lord and Holy Spirit to disclose the meaning/hidden message behind each (whether it aligns with what I already sensed or not).

Some visions/dreams point to what has happened, what is occurring in the present, or what is to come. As the Lord reveals, the more I intercede. As things have manifested in the natural, I have been able to record my level of accuracy regarding the interpretations of the vision/dreams. The accuracy is important because it allows you to pray specific prayers as opposed to praying amiss.

Then, you can confidently war in intercession (especially if it is a situation/event/demonic plot that needs to be hindered and rendered both defenseless and inoperable.

As an intercessor, please be sure to apply these pointers when you begin to have visions and dreams:

1. Always keep a journal and some type of writing technology on your nightstand or near your bed so you can record a vision or dream, as soon as you are awakened, or as soon as you recall it.

2. Write down everything you saw and what was said in the vision/dream.

3. Record the major things that stood out to you.

4. Jot down what you think the vision/dream is about. If you have absolutely no clue, that is perfectly fine.

5. Whether you think you know what it is about or not, saturate the contents of the vision/dream in prayer. Ask the Lord for revelation and interpretation.

6. You may want to refer to a dream dictionary to guide you with some of the symbolisms. I recommend that you do not depend solely on them. They are merely a guide. The Holy Spirit is the best pilot who can steer you down the road to revelation.

7. Scripture says in the multitude of counselors there is safety. You may want to consider sharing your dream with your senior pastor, or a trusted, experienced leader who can assist in interpreting and unraveling your vision/dream.

8. Jot down some prayer points/prayer bullets that you would like to target concerning the vision/dream.

---

9. Some visions/dreams may require weeks, months, or even years of intercession. Use the revelations about your visions/dreams to intercede, intercede, and intercede some more until the Lord releases you from that specific assignment.

I leave you with this quote:

Remember, we are not seeking experiences, we are seeking a pure heart. We are not running after visions; we desire holiness. Even as the supernatural realm was an expected phenomenon in the primitive Church, so also was purity the expected condition in their hearts. Therefore do not be as the foolish ones who seek visions.

*You must seek sanctification, and when you are ready, if God wills, He shall speak to you in supernatural ways (see Acts 2:17-18). Do not seek to conjure up an "experience" with Jesus; seek to have a clean heart, allowing Christ to examine and purge you daily. And as He washes you with His Word and chastens you with His holiness, He will draw you into His presence. He will open your eyes to "things without and things within."-**Francis Frangipane***

—

Chapter Five:

"YOU MEAN I HAVE TO FIGHT?"

While in a deep sleep, I felt someone tug on my arm with an urgency for me to awaken. I was really battling exiting my comfortable bed. Then, as clear as day, I heard someone shout a man's name (Mark to be exact). I jumped out of my sleep. I quickly glanced at the clock which displayed a little after two in the morning. I was physically exhausted so it took me a minute to enter my prayer closet. Once there, I knelt down and paused. I waited, and waited, and waited some more with a temptation to dash right back under the warm covers. Thankfully, I didn't. Then, the directives came. The Lord communicated to me that Mark was a missionary stationed in Africa and that he was ready to throw in the towel.

Now I have never met Mark. Frankly, I don't know the man. However, I was expected to intercede on his behalf and that is what I proceeded to do. After praying for Mark, I began to stand in the gap for all missionaries and everyone in ministry that felt like giving up. I cried out for God to send the Aarons and Hurs to uphold their arms. I wept for those who were dedicated and involved in ministry for the building up of God's house; yet, their own households were in complete shambles. I pleaded for a release of finances and resources. With the help of Holy Spirit praying through me, I addressed the foul spirits of depression, hopelessness, suicide, lack, fear, and failure. I wailed for their soundness of mind, for strength against burn-out, for rejuvenation, a wind of refreshing to blow upon them, an unleashing of angels to fight on their behalf, and for God to intervene.

As I interceded, I felt the burdens. I took on the weight of Mark and others' discouragement. "No!" I screamed. These apostles, prophets, pastors, teachers, evangelists, worship leaders, Sunday School teachers, ushers, missionaries, song writers, and many more that work tirelessly in God's kingdom cannot give up. They just can't! Someone is inspired by their lives.

The salvation of lost souls is dependent upon these men and women of God. Someone's breakthrough will manifest as a result of their consistency and faithfulness.

That morning, the spiritual warfare was intense. War had broken out in the spirit realm. A mission was at hand. I was summoned just like a soldier is summoned when deployed for duty. Life or death was at stake. I was awakened and alerted to contend for life. An intercessor was needed to assist in manifesting victory in the natural. I rolled up my pajama sleeves and climbed into the boxing ring with the enemy and his goons. At times, my knees began to weaken but I kept bombarding heaven without relenting. The tiredness that I felt earlier had eventually left. I kept fighting. Jehovah Sabaoth (The Lord of Hosts) and the heavenly army of angels had my back. That's the confidence that I had. I was not in this fight alone. However, the Lord needed my cooperation. Through intercession, I bit, kicked, punched, scratched, and clawed away at the kingdom of darkness. I didn't stop until I felt a release to do so.

When I was younger, my biological father always advised me and my siblings to avoid fights as much as we possibly could. He said if someone picked on us or struck us, we were to seek out a teacher/an adult and report the incident. Under no circumstances were we allowed to engage in a brawl. For the most part, I can say I was a very obedient child. I didn't fight, and I rarely got into trouble. One day at school, all that my father told me went straight out the window. All because of a tall, string bean looking boy. One day, our regular teacher was absent. Unfortunately, we were assigned a substitute teacher who simply didn't care and possessed no classroom management skills. The students decided to take full advantage of this.

I refused to participate in the collaborative chaos that ensued so I sat quietly at my desk and proceeded to read a book. For his enjoyment, string bean decided he was going to launch spit balls. The problem with this was that the spitballs were aimed at a specific target. You guessed correctly. I happened to be that poor target.

Despite my annoyance, I stayed at my seat and politely asked toothpick to stop. He refused. The spitballs only grew larger, were ejected faster than I could say my name, and found their resting place on top of me. I finally decided to get out of my chair, walked directly over to string bean, looked him square in the eyes, raised my voice, and demanded that I be left alone. While he remained seated (obviously surprised and displeased by my confrontation), gave me one slap across the face that sent my glasses flying across the room. He struck me so hard that my glasses broke. That did it for me! I became enraged. All I could think about was the butt whooping that awaited me when my father found out that my glasses were shattered (dad had already complained that he didn't have a lot of money so I had better take good care of my glasses). The thought of me having to tell my father that he would have to replace my glasses caused tears to stream down my face.

The sleeping beast in me was now awakened. I clenched both fists, and when string bean saw how infuriated I was, he immediately stood up. That posed a serious problem because he was way taller than I was. I had to tilt my head back to glance up at the towering giant. As they say, "Where there's a will, there's a way." I mounted a chair which elevated my height above his. I pounded away senselessly and beat him to a lifeless pulp. I was determined to draw blood. If he never saw crazy, I promise he came face to face with her that day. The battering ram was unleashed through my persistent fists. The substitute teacher finally decided to intervene and had to literally peel me off of him.

—

To make a long story short, we were both taken to the Dean's office. I was not suspended due to an impeccable academic record and no previous altercations. The Dean issued a verbal warning and proceeded to contact my father. Although dad was upset about me fighting and him having to spend money that was budgeted for something else, he went ahead and replaced my glasses. As tall and threatening as he was, skinny Goliath never messed with me again, nor did any other student at that school.

What's my purpose in sharing these personal stories? Well, there are a few things I'd like to extrapolate here. For starters, you're in for a fight. Although I was not a fighter and neither was I looking for a fight, when push came to shove, I did what I had to do to defend myself against a bully. Since I never fought before this incident, how did I know what to do? I pulled on my natural instincts as well as anything I may have ever heard or seen about fighting. Something rose up within me and my gut sense of how to handle the problem just automatically kicked in. That day, combat met combat, fight confronted fight, and trouble encountered trouble. The next thing is that what we learn in the natural, does not always apply spiritually. My dad told me never to fight. However, as a Christian and especially as an intercessor, combat automatically comes with the territory, as pointed out in the first account mentioned above. Heaven enlists you with or without your permission.

It's equivalent to getting a job and all the requirements are already laid out for you. Well, once you're born again, you've registered to fight. Yes, I know it's unsettling. No, I don't mean fighting with your fists. We cannot fight a spiritual battle or war with natural abilities. It would be foolish to do so because we don't war against what we see but against what we don't see.

Ephesians 6:11-13 *(NKJV)* says *"Put on the whole armor of God, that you may be able to stand against the wiles of the devil. For we do not wrestle against flesh and blood, but against principalities, against powers, against the rulers of the darkness of this age, against spiritual hosts of wickedness in the heavenly places. Therefore take up the whole armor of God, that you may be able to withstand in the evil day, and having done all, to stand."*

This is a wrestling match that takes place in prayer, on bended knees. At times you will get a break between rounds but it's an ongoing fight. The only way of escape is natural death. Please understand that this is not optional. Whether you want to or not, whether you feel like it or not, you'd better gear up. We have to get used to spiritual warfare. Spiritual warfare is real and is unavoidable. What in fact is spiritual warfare? It's exactly what it sounds like; it's war in the spirit. It can be defined as the actions involved in opposing or standing against the forces and plans of the kingdom of darkness. It is certainly not a match for the timid, weak hearted, or the cowardly. I know many Christians who dread having to engage in warfare. I used to be one of them. The enemy has a field day with the lives of these Christians because by not fighting, he knows they've accepted defeat. These Christians are an easy target and the devil goes in for the kill. *John 10:10* *(NKJV)* Jesus exclaims *"The thief does not come except to steal, and to kill, and to destroy. I have come that they may have life, and that they may have it more abundantly."*

Have you ever watched a wrestling match where on one side of the ring was a big, well-built individual, yet on the other side of the ring was a small, scrawny looking person? You shake your head in disbelief because you know the opponents are not fairly/equally matched from the start. Often times, the well-built individual tends to grab the upper-hand early during the struggle and usually wins the combat.

When we choose not to fight or are too afraid to attack back, the enemy gets the upper-hand and it becomes more challenging to break free of his choke hold. On this Christian journey, you must contend for yourself, everyone, and everything attached to you. Other times, you will be battling on behalf of others whether you know them personally or not. As intercessors, when your schedule is divinely interrupted like I mentioned at the beginning of this chapter, often times, you are being summoned to do warfare for others.

There is good news! If you are enlisted as a soldier in the army of the Lord, He has already equipped you. God always equips those He calls. You need not fear for God has not given you a spirit of fear *(2 Timothy 1:17)*. What's essential is preparation. The question is, are you up for the fight? As an intercessor, you don't necessarily get to pick and choose who and what to stand in the gap for. God issues the assignments and burdens. Even when you don't feel like it, when heaven dials your number for you to stand in the gap, it is your responsibility to do so. If you have the heart and mind of Christ, it's difficult to hear about a dire situation and NOT intervene in prayer. For example, you may report to work one morning only to learn that your co-worker was involved in a tragic car accident and they are now on life support. You will automatically feel a tug to pray for your coworker because it is part of your spiritual DNA to do so.

An intercessor would never say "Although it's a disheartening plight for my coworker to be in, I didn't necessarily get the burden from God to pray for him. Plus, he was mean and never treated me right anyway." I guarantee you that a police officer who takes his job seriously will feel compelled to act and get involved if he witnesses a robbery even though he may be off-duty.

The call to protect citizens and the community he serves is so imbedded in his bloodstream, conscience, and character that he cannot turn a blind eye whether in or out of uniform. We are our brother's keeper. Intercessors must be prepared in season and out of season. The plain truth is that there is rarely an off season for an intercessor, but be not dismayed as to how you are going to fight. Christians possess various weapons in their spiritual arsenal appropriate for warfare. I name a few below:

1. The name of Jesus Christ the Messiah- Scripture says that at the name of Jesus, every knee shall bow and every tongue shall confess that He is Lord. His name stands alone and is powerful.

2. The anointing oil- This was a covering and ointment. Scripturally, it represents the Holy Spirit, endowment of power, authority, and it enables the believer to carry out their God given assignments.

3. The blood of Jesus- There is resurrection, reviving, restoring, and replenishing power in the blood of Jesus. We understand that it is by the shed blood of Jesus. Even in the Old Testament, the children of Israel were instructed to place the blood on their doorposts and the lintels of their houses so that they would not be subject to plagues or death (Read *Exodus 12:1-13*). As believers, we are to apply confess the blood every opportunity that we are afforded. Plead the blood over everyone and everything connected to you. The blood of Jesus Christ will attack all that is out of alignment in your life.

4. Angelic assistance- All throughout scripture, angels were dispatched to assist the people of God when they went to battle, were weak in strength, needed provision, and sought guidance. Don't hesitate to ask the Lord to

—

unleash warring angels, ministering angels, and guardian angels on yours and others behalf.

5. The Word of God- This is one of the most powerful weapons. Do you remember after Jesus fasted for forty days and forty nights, he was led into the wilderness to be tempted by Satan, for every lie the devil dished out, Jesus blocked it with TRUTH. Jesus said "It is written, it is written, it is written." If Jesus had to quote the word, how much more do we? *Isaiah 55:10, 11* says *"For as the rain comes down, and the snow from heaven, and do not return there, but water the earth, and make it bring forth and bud, that it may give seed to the sower and bread to the eater, so shall My word be that goes forth from My mouth: It shall not return to Me void, But it shall accomplish what I please, And it shall prosper in the thing for which I sent it." Psalm 138:2 "I will worship toward Your holy temple, And praise Your name For Your lovingkindness and Your truth; For You have magnified Your word above all Your name."* When you intercede, remind God of what He said. God honors His word.

6. Worship- There are times you go to intercede and the Lord will prompt you to utilize the technology of worship instead. More is accomplished in worship than we actually comprehend. Principalities are put to flight and the walls of Jericho crumble as we lift up the name of the Lord.

7. Unity/Agreement- Much is conquered in intercession when there is unity among believers. Jesus said where two or three are gathered in His name, He is there, in the midst of them, to do their bidding. It is always beneficial for an intercessor to get another intercessor to stand in agreement with them on behalf of someone or a certain situation. There are times for confidentiality reasons or

when a sudden burden comes, one may not be able to do so. However, believe that the Father, Son, and Holy Spirit is present when you pray.

8. Prayer- The Bible puts it plainly in *Matthew 7:7-11 (NKJV) Ask, and it will be given to you; seek, and you will find; knock, and it will be opened to you. For everyone who asks receives, and he who seeks finds, and to him who knocks it will be opened. Or what man is there among you who, if his son asks for bread, will give him a stone? Or if he asks for a fish, will he give him a serpent? If you then, being evil, know how to give good gifts to your children, how much more will your Father who is in heaven give good things to those who ask Him!* Prayer is a spiritual key to obtain answers. Intercessors must utilize their key to decree and declare, bind, loose, lock, unlock, root out, pull down, destroy, and throw down, build and to plant in the spirit.

9. Fasting- Adds fuel and power to your prayers. Jesus told the disciples that there are certain principalities and demons that are not displaced unless one prays **and** fast *(Mark 9:25-29)*. Remember, two are always better than one. Scripture says one shall chase a thousand, but two shall chase ten thousand *(Deuteronomy 32:30)*. Fasting is absolutely essential in the life of every believer, let alone an intercessor. In *Matthew 6:16-18* the Lord tells us that **when** we fast, we are to do it unto the Lord. He doesn't say **if** we fast.

10. Holy Spirit- There are numerous functions of Holy Spirit. I will only mention three here that are applicable to intercession. First and foremost, Holy Spirit is a revealer of secrets. When you remain sensitive to Holy Spirit, you will not be in the dark as you intercede. *John 16:13 (NKJV) However, when He, the Spirit of truth, has come, He will guide you into all truth; for He will*

not speak on His own authority, but whatever He hears He will speak; and He will tell you things to come. Secondly, Holy Spirit also prays through believers when they don't know what to pray. **Romans 8:26, 27 (NKJV)** *Likewise the Spirit also helps in our weaknesses. For we do not know what we should pray for as we ought, but the Spirit Himself makes intercession for us with groanings which cannot be uttered. Now He who searches the hearts knows what the mind of the Spirit is, because He makes intercession for the saints according to the will of God.* Thirdly, Holy Spirit is a Helper. Another word for helper is "comforter" or "legal aid". Therefore, Holy Spirit is one who assists us. **John 14:16 (NKJV)** *And I will pray the Father, and He will give you another Helper, that He may abide with you forever— [17] the Spirit of truth, whom the world cannot receive, because it neither sees Him nor knows Him; but you know Him, for He dwells with you and will be in you.*

A few helpful tips to keep in mind before engaging in spiritual warfare:

- Ensure that you are prayed up and are completely robed in battle gear. Do not go into combat unprepared. Understand that intercession is a spiritual activity and once you begin to engage, you are literally entering the spirit realm. **Ephesians 6:13-18 (NKJV)** *"Therefore take up the whole armor of God, that you may be able to withstand in the evil day, and having done all, to stand. Stand therefore, having girded your waist with truth, having put on the breastplate of righteousness, and having shod your feet with the preparation of the gospel of peace; above all, taking the shield of faith with which you will be able to quench all the fiery darts of the wicked one. And take the helmet of salvation, and the sword of the Spirit, which is the word of God; praying always with all prayer and supplication in the Spirit,*

71

being watchful to this end with all perseverance and supplication for all the saints."

- Be yourself when you pray. Never try to imitate someone else. Now, when you first begin to train as an intercessor, God will place intercessory role models who will mentor you. You may find yourself praying as they do, mimicking the same tone they use to pray, or even doing similar hand gestures. The more you pray, you will begin to find your own tone and style. Become comfortable in your own skin. You are uniquely you for a reason. Become the Intercessor you were meant to be.

Now I'd like to issue a warning for new babes in Christ or even those that are new to intercession. It is imperative that you drive your vehicle in your assigned lane and that you understand and are honest about your rank. We have new Christians that are going out and purchasing John Eckhardt's book Prayer That Route Demons or Dr. Cindy Trimm's CD titled The Atomic Power of Prayer and they repeat these prayers verbatim. Apostle John Eckhardt and Dr. Cindy Trimm are notable, highly respected, and anointed men and women of God. Their resources are an absolute blessing to the Body of Christ. When it involves purchasing and reading some of their materials, that is perfectly fine. However, when it comes to reciting someone else's prayers verbatim, that is a different ballgame altogether.

One must be extremely careful and discerning. Very few Christians understand the power of rank. Apostle John Eckhardt and Dr. Cindy Trimm are GENERALS at what

---

they do. They underwent a process to get to where they are currently. For example, in education a student doesn't get skipped to grade five without having completed grades one, two, three, and four. One is expected to graduate from high school prior to any College admission. For an administrator, it is highly unlikely that you can hold the title of Principal without having first served as an Assistant Principal. Levels must be mastered.

- Rank is your status, power, authority, and title within a system or organization. There is rank in the military. We also clearly see the principle of rank within the police force. The order and natural progression within that organization is first Officer/Deputy/Corporal, second is the Detective, third is the Sergeant, then Lieutenant, next we progress to Captain, afterwards Major, then Colonel, next Deputy Chief, then Sheriff, and finally the Police Commissioner. Therefore, it would be foolish to think that a plainly clothed officer has the same rank/authority as the Police Commissioner. He does not. As it is in the natural world, so it is in the realm of the spirit. Please understand that there is rank among the angels, demons, principalities, and powers. Rank recognizes rank. When you have an opportunity, please read *Jude 1:9* and *Daniel 10:10-20*. Just briefly in *Jude 1:9*, we see Michael the Archangel stood against Satan and contended for the resurrected body of Moses. In *Daniel 10:10-20* Michael the Archangel was dispatched to war against the Prince of Persia. In the bible, Michael is the Archangel. The word Archangel literally means "chief of the angels". This was a clear indication that Michael was the commander, leader, or chief over the other angels. On the opposite end, we understand that Satan is the captain over all the powers of darkness *(Revelation 12:7-9)*. He gives the orders and his commands are carried out by those under him. As mentioned earlier,

---

intercession is a spiritual activity that involves the spirit world and spirit beings. Remember we wrestle not against flesh and blood.

The point that I am trying to make here is that a new Christian or someone who does not understand the world of intercession should not be reciting prayers that distinguished, high ranking generals in the kingdom of God have the authority to pray. Dr. Cindy Trimm has an elevated rank in the spirit. When she prays, she wars against high ranking principalities and demons. If you decide you are going to copy her prayers, then be prepared to face the same high ranking powers of darkness that Dr. Trimm deals with. The issue is Dr. Trimm may have the authority to withstand them, you on the other hand may not. Christians who go around echoing warfare prayers without wisdom and revelation, are often left scratching their heads when all hell breaks loose in their lives. They intercede for someone, then spend the next week laid up in a hospital bed or experience several car wrecks in a matter of months. The reason behind this is that they did not have the rank to thwart the backlashes of the enemy. Now the more training, insight, wisdom, and practice you gain as an intercessor, your intercessory muscles will begin to build/expand. You will notice a shift in your prayers. Your spiritual power and rank will automatically catapult. Until then, try your best to remain in your lane and exercise the spiritual authority you've been rendered.

Chapter Six:

ABANDONED LOVE

What's love got to do with it? Well, the creator of the universe thought that love or the lack of it has everything to do with everything. So much so that His very essence and DNA is love, that's how important it is to God. *1 John 4:8* proclaims that God is love. Since we are made in the likeness and image of God, man is a magnet when it comes to love. It is mere nonsense when someone says "I don't need anybody." That is a cover-up for some pain that lies deep within. Everyone may not know how to give love or how to receive love, but whether people admit it or not, everyone wants to be loved. Love is ancient and yet one of the most potent medicines in existence.

An entire chapter in the Bible is devoted to love and it appears to be the running theme throughout scripture. *1 Corinthians 13: 4-8* reads *Love suffers long and is kind; love does not envy; love does not parade itself; is not puffed up; does not behave rudely;, does not seek its own, is not provoked, thinks no evil; does not rejoice in iniquity, but rejoices in the truth; bears all things, hopes all things, endures all things, love never fails…*

Wait, did you say love never fails? If love is so great, why is it that those who are supposed to love you, or that you are supposed to love end up hurting each other? If my mother loved me, she would not have died so young, leaving me unshielded and having to fend for myself for the majority of my life. If he loved me and my family, he would not have molested me. If my coworker loved me, they would not have been jealous, nor would they have backstabbed me the way they did. The truth is God's love never fails and no matter what we experience in life, we must believe this truth.

I got saved at the age of fourteen. Two years later, I fell madly in love with this unsaved, handsome, Jamaican stud. Lord knows I loved me some him (at least that is what my mind and heart told me every day).

—

Two years later, I trusted him enough to let him touch not just my heart but my body. That is when he and I had our first sexual encounter. I loved God but just didn't know better not to fornicate. Then, I remember changing the church that I usually attended. At this new church in New York, the worship and word was unlike anything I had experienced before. Everything tugged at my heart strings. The tangible presence of God was all over me every time I entered that sanctuary, and even lingered with me when I went home.

Now you can imagine that I began to grow by leaps and bounds in my walk with the Lord. I just hungered for more of God. One day, I was having a conversation with the Lord and was expressing my love for Him. The Lord basically gave me an ultimatum. He said "It's him or it's Me!" I was still in a relationship with my gorgeous, unsaved, Jamaican fella. Looking back, I believe he was an idol in my life. While I worshipped God, I also worshipped him. So with the Lord's proposal, I had a decision to make. Guess who I chose? The Lord of course! I cried many days for my jerk chicken. I truly loved him, but God was calling me higher, and my swift and appropriate response was crucial. I had to abandon the first man I ever loved to pursue God. That was very painful, but I eventually got over it and got over him. After Mr. Jamaica, I proceeded to date two individuals. My relationship with these two guys impacted me significantly.

After giving up my Jamaican boyfriend, I finally met a Christian guy that I was very much into. He was a youth Pastor at his church. We became very good friends and our conversations were centered on God and scripture. We prayed often with and for each other. He traveled a lot on ministry related trips. Whenever he checked in, I was the second person he called after he spoke to his mother. That is just how close we were.

We often talked on the phone for countless hours (sometimes at 1 a.m., 2 a.m., and 3 a.m. in the morning). Our friendship was real and pure. I cared for him deeply but never divulged my true feelings to him. By the way he treated me, I could tell that he felt the same way. Just neither one of us had the courage to do anything about it.

One day we were having a discussion, then all of a sudden, we both became silent. My friend seemed to be wrestling with something he wanted to ask me. He said "Joey (that's what he used to call me, but my real nickname is Jojo) are you a virgin?" That wasn't the question I was expecting. I thought he was going to ask me out on a date. I responded truthfully and said "No" Lord, if you could see the expression on his face. His eyes turned red as though he wanted to cry and it looked like someone knocked the wind out of him. He probably thought to himself "She is such a sweet Christian girl. How could she not be a virgin?" You see, he was a virgin, and was looking for a relationship with a virgin girl. I definitely came up short (thanks to jerk chicken). While he didn't stop being my friend, he immediately abandoned any idea of us being together. I was hurt, bitter, resentful, devastated, enraged, you name it! A few years later, I had to endure the pain of seeing him marry someone else. Today, he is a well-known, integrous, influential pastor, and still friends.

Just a few years later, a Christian guy at my church pursued me for eight months before I agreed to date him. Boy was he on fire for God. His love for the Lord was contagious. Eventually, I fell in love with him. In our many conversations, we both expressed we wanted to spend the rest of our lives together. One day he proposed, I accepted. We went to premarital counseling, received the blessing of our pastors, friends, and family, and wed about two years later.

The presence of the Lord was so tangible at our wedding. Many people told us they attended very few weddings where God showed up the way He did. Aside from kissing and holding hands (it was not easy at all), I can honestly say we waited patiently to have our first sexual encounter on our wedding night. Hooray! I did it God's way! We will now ride into the sunset and live happily ever after, right?

Dead wrong! Ten years, and two kids later, my marriage fell apart. It was a train wreck waiting to happen because both of us were two broken individuals with a lot of emotional baggage from our past. We just didn't know how to make the other okay. He sought comfort, love, and attention elsewhere, while I buried myself in work, ministry, and the kids. I thought I was a loving wife, I tried my best but my best was not good enough. We ended up divorcing. I was left with a mortgage, two cars, our two kids, and a mountain of bills. I ended up losing the house to foreclosure and almost everything else, except my beautiful, precious children.

The circumstances under which my ex-husband and I parted was so unfair. By far I was not perfect but I went to work, cooked, cleaned, took care of the kids, attended church consistently, prayed, and fasted. How could this happen to me? Where are you God? How dare you let this happen and let him get away with murdering my heart? I became pissed, enraged, and thought I was going to lose my righteous mind. My hair started falling out, I lost weight, I became depressed, and I secretly harbored hate in my heart. I was a real face behind the well- known movie Diary of a Mad Black Woman, except without a charming Shemar Moore to come to the rescue. I call all of the above ABANDONED LOVE!

The experiences I share in the book account for 1% of all that I have endured in my life. I thank the Lord that I never lost my mind even after having gone to hell and back.

Today, I am in contact with my ex for the sake of our children. We are cordial and civil with one another. I honestly pray the best for him. No, I don't ask the Lord to break his legs or rip his heart out anymore (no matter how bad people hurt you, witchcraft prayers are NOT the will of the Lord). As a Christian, I was always a praying woman, but it was not until I hit rock bottom that my intercessory well truly uncapped. A tsunami of intercessory prayers began to manifest in unusual ways. I began to have compassion for others, truly feel their pain, weep over them, and war on their behalf. At times, it's like I want to grab the devil by his neck, and squeeze the life out of him, to prevent others from experiencing the years of pain I had to deal with. God began to reveal Himself to me in mind blowing ways. He began to strategically position me for ministry above what I could have asked or imagined. He has healed me of the hatred, rage, depression, resentment and more. Now why would I possibly take up all this space to talk about some of my past experiences with love?

I recently ministered at a gala called "All Bottled Up" and had the assignment of interceding for, prophesying over, and helping individuals to release years of pain that they were holding on to. All the individuals were Christians, who loved God, but were sadly bound. We have to understand that it is unwise and outright foolish to pour new wine into old wineskins. We want to be used by God and do all these great exploits (all EXTERNAL things). Life's lessons teach us that the external will quickly fail to gratify if the INTERNAL has not been dealt with and made new. If we are to be effective intercessors, we have to look in the mirror first and allow God to work on us. We never want to pray from a wounded or bitter place. Those become infected prayers. I will share part of the message I delivered at "All Bottle Up". Perhaps, this will help a hurting intercessor who desires to break free.

- A bottle is merely a vessel meant to contain/hold specific things for significant times.

- What a bottle contains indicates its value. If I am into perfume, the fragrance **Beautiful**, by Estee Lauder, will be worth more to me than a bottle of Nyquil. If someone drinks 3 or more bottles of Coca Cola per day to get their caffeine fix, we can deduce that the bottle of soda is more meaningful to them than a bottle of Apple Cider Vinegar. Suffice to say that the owner of a particular bottle determines its value.

- The contents of a bottle also point to its purpose. If I have a container of syrup, I am not going to use it to lotion my skin, but to drizzle all over my pancakes, because that's what it's made for. If I own a bottle of perfume, I am not going to drink it if I am thirsty, but use it to make body smell wonderful.

- Whether it is a bottle of lotion, perfume, water etc. the contents are useless until they are poured out. If the substances are not released at some point, it is safe to acknowledge that the contents remain "all bottled up".

- When and if you decide to dispense the elements of a flask, you must be careful to avoid sloppy and nasty spills.

Please understand that you too are a vessel, so I dare pose these questions to you:
- **What is your value?**
- **Who do you allow to determine your value?**
- **What is your purpose?**
- **What are you carrying?**
- **What are you pouring out?**

What are you carrying and what are you pouring out?

> Many of us because of the bad experiences we've gone through or have endured in life are carrying invisible suitcases with our shattered hearts, emotional instability, wounds, hurt, fears, insecurities, traumas, weaknesses, and temptations that no one sees. The Bible tells us that God desires truth in the inward parts. But we lie and make people think we're happy. We smile and say that things are fine and that is the farthest thing from the truth.

> At times we are cognizant that the load we bear is heavy and we get tired of hauling it around. Lord knows we've tried to unpack our issues. But just when we think we're good, a rug gets pulled from under our feet. Here comes another fool, yet another disappointment, another liar, another ungrateful person, another abuser, another irritating co-worker, an obnoxious boss. We've unpacked, only to pack again and we become disgruntled. We carry fears, tears, pain, rage, hurt, dirt and much more.

> We travel from place to place with all this internal stuff "all bottled up". We often fail to realize that every container is a certain size, a certain length, width, and height, which all equates to the vessel's capacity. Some bottles can only hold 6 ounces, others can hold, 8, 16, 24 ounces and more.

> What happens when you've reached your capacity? For our topic and context, your capacity is your ability to

withstand the pressure and weight of rejection, abandonment, betrayal, abuse, pain, disappointment, loss etc. ***Imagine someone holding a bottle of Coca-Cola and they keep shaking it fiercely.

While you entertain that visual in your head, say to yourself:
- Why did my sister have to die so early?
- Say one more stupid thing to me
- Lie to me one more time
- Talk about me again behind my back
- You've stolen from me far too many times
- How many times must I get a phone call from your school?
- Why do you always misinterpret my words and actions?
- Cheat on me with another side chick
- I'm so sick and tired of your I'm sorry only for you to turn around and do the same thing over and over. You are nothing more than a repeat offender.
- **"Don't push me cause I'm close to the edge, I'm trying not to lose my head!"**

➢ When you are shaken too much, whatever is in you will inevitably discharge. Did you ever see what happens to a bottle of soda when it experiences turbulence? Pressure from within begins to mount. The tension builds and builds until it climaxes. As soon as the cap comes off, all you hear is "pssssshhhhhh". There's a volcanic eruption.

➢ When we fail to properly release our years upon years of hurt, loss, pain, defeat, anger, unforgiveness, resentment,

—

83

and bitterness over the love we didn't receive, what someone did to us, and what they said to us, we too will eventually snap and explode. God helps anyone standing in our path when we do so. Please hear me! You can try to bury your stuff, but when a tumultuous wind and storm arises, the surface leaves, paper, sticks, and rocks gets blown to the side and what really lies in the belly of the earth hits the surface and becomes exposed. It will rear its ugly head when you least expect it. On your job, in your marriage, in ministry, and towards your kids. Even innocent bystanders become targets.

➤ What I just mentioned is a clear depiction of vessels of dishonor. When you transport and inappropriately release all that junk that's been in your trunk, you dishonor God, you disgrace people in your life, you diminish your value, clog your true purpose, and delay or forfeit divine destiny.

➤ This is not an exhaustive list but I'll give you about 11 appropriate ways to release years of pain:
  1. Prayer- Because nothing happens until and unless we pray
  2. Fasting-Jesus said some things (such as demonic spirits) don't come out until we fast and pray.
  3. Counseling- Preferably spiritual counselors but there are experts out in the world that can provide counseling as well
  4. Consistently Reading- Meditating on, and Decreeing and Declaring God's word over yourself

5. Renewing your mind- Every battle that is won or lost is first fought in the mind. Again that's where the daily washing of the Word comes in as stated in *Ephesians 5:26*
6. The Blood- Applying the power of The Blood of Jesus
7. Forgiveness- Whether you actually turn it in or not, writing a letter to the individual(s) who hurt you (expressing what they did and that you choose to forgive them). Get it off your chest
8. Communication- Having an actual conversation with the individual(s)-use wisdom here. Sometimes that is not always the best decision
9. Deliverance- Receiving deliverance and healing
10. Let go- Decide to just lay it down and let it go. You can't carry luggage unless you first pick it up. It's time to drop it
11. The Prophetic- Prophetic word/impartation can break things off your life

God determines your value

➤ God has already determined your value. But you must cooperate with Him by walking it out by faith. According to *Genesis 1:27* you were made in the likeness and image of Almighty God. Then *Psalm 139: 13-14* reads *"For You formed my inward parts; You covered me in my mother's womb. I will praise You, for I am fearfully and wonderfully made; Marvelous are Your works, And that my soul knows very well."*

> You are extremely valuable to the Lord. He makes no mistakes and He doesn't create trash. Before the foundations of the world, God ordained your very existence. And it did not include you walking around with years of demonic debris. By no means is that the perfect and beautiful image of your God.

Your Ultimate Purpose

> The release of all interior poison is important but should not be looked upon as an end product/destination. Since you were made to glorify God, He has a plan and assignment for your life. There's another level in your finances, education, business, relationships, ministry, gifting, and calling that is yet to be conquered. He wants to use you to advance His agenda here on earth. So take the cap off, get unclogged so He can fill you with His ideas, give you His mind, His heart, His wisdom, His strategies, His power, and His love.

> Don't you just desire better and more for your life? Instead of vessels of dishonor, we can be vessels of honor, vessels of gold that release a sweet smelling aroma traveling up to the nostrils of God when we are poured out by Him.

In summary, we want to be new vessels of glory and honor for God. This will involve being intentional about releasing all the internal toxins that are bottled up within us.

- You've endured hell and high water but there's no testimony without the test, no crown without the cross.

- The anointing costs and you've paid dearly in your lifetime (sleepless nights, distrust of others, emotional eating, weight gain, hair loss, loss of relationships, foreclosures, repossessions, sickness in your body, indecisiveness, depression, and the list goes on). **Stop paying your pain and become debt free!**

- Today, take a stand and say "Enough is Enough!" Make the decision and declaration to let go of every ounce of pain, hurt, rage, unforgiveness, bitterness, and carry it no more. Be made whole again!

Chapter Seven:

"ARE YOU WATCHING?"

There was one particular week in 2016 that I kept picking up school shootings in my spirit. One afternoon, the burden was so strong I had to stop everything. It was so urgent. I quickly alerted all the leaders at our church and asked them to bombard heaven. My specific request was that the Lord would expose all plots by the enemy to attack students and school staff, and that all perpetrators would be apprehended. Within two days, we heard about two attempted school shootings at two different locations in our city. Thankfully the suspects in both incidents were captured before any lives were destroyed.

Another time, I kept seeing suicidal faces among believers in the Body of Christ. I informed our intercessors and they began to war, attacking every depressive spirit, demolishing mental strongholds, and covering the minds of the saints. That same week, many people came forward confessing that there was an all-out attack by hell to take their lives. That yoke was broken in Jesus name. Sadly, we heard of reports from our local news channels of individuals at schools or at their places of work that did in fact commit suicide. We were pretty sure the number would have been higher had the saints not interceded.

In another case, a friend of mine kept dropping in my spirit for about two weeks. Finally, one morning I dreamt about her. In the dream, her face revealed she was in extreme agony. She was seated on a chair, her legs were open like in a V-like position, and two demons (one on the left and one on the right) were pulling at her feet specifically by the heels. Immediately after the dream, I jumped up. I looked at the clock and it was a little after six in the morning. I entered my prayer closet and began to intercede for my friend right away. I knew this meant warfare. I prayed primarily in the Holy Ghost. When you don't know what to pray as you ought, Holy Spirit will pray through you. I bombarded heaven and kept going. I could literally feel the pain that my friend was in.

—

I relented not, until I felt a release to stop praying. Afterwards I proceeded to go back to bed.

Later during the day, I was prompted to call my friend. As soon as she picked up the phone, she expressed how thrilled she was that I called. She conveyed that I hadn't the slightest idea what she had been going through. I asked her to please share. My friend proceeded to explain. She described how for the past two weeks, she was experiencing excruciating pain in her feet. She went to the doctor, but they could not pinpoint what the source of the pain was (obviously because the pain had a spiritual origin, not a natural one, however, there was a physical manifestation of what was transpiring in the spirit).

She kept changing her shoes in an effort to alleviate the discomfort she was feeling. Absolutely nothing seemed to bring relief. My friend then articulated that all of a sudden, that morning, the pain in her feet just vanished. I listened attentively as she spoke. When she was finished, I felt led to share with her the dream that I had and how I was prompted to stand in the gap for her that very morning. We both began to praise the Lord. We spent a significant amount of time just worshipping God over the phone. We were thankful for the faithfulness of God. In a dream, the Lord pinpointed what was causing the pain in her feet and used someone to stand on her behalf via the engines of intercession. After our outbursts of praise and worship, my friend and I continued to converse about different matters that was going on in her life. It was apparent that the enemy was seeking to derail what God was doing in her life and ministry. We discussed the significance of someone's feet and heels. In *Luke 10:19*, Jesus told the disciples that they were given authority by Him to trample on serpents and scorpions. In scripture the feet or heels represent dominion, authority, and power.

We see this portrayed in *Genesis 25: 24-34* regarding the twins Jacob and Esau. Although Esau was the firstborn, Jacob grabbed his heel as he came out of the womb. It was a prophetic action signifying he would take what belonged to his brother. We later read that Jacob indeed went on to steal his brother's birthright. Therefore, it was clear Satan's scheme was to paralyze my friend both in the natural and spiritual so that she could not exercise her power and authority. Once a Christian's power and authority is taken away or hindered, they cannot possess what God has ordained for them to inherit.

There was so much revelation as we dialogued one with another. I also had the opportunity to share what was going on in my life. We both encouraged each other. I just love what the Word of God says when it asserts that iron sharpeneth iron, so a friend the countenance of their friend *(Proverbs 27:17)*. After our long discussion, we said our goodbyes and hung up the phone. About an hour after I hung up the phone, Holy Spirit brought something to my remembrance. I recalled the time that I was abruptly awakened to intercede for my friend. It was a little after six in the morning. I was reminded that during that specific prayer watch, healing is accessed.

The Lord orchestrated that intercession would go forth for my friend so that the demons would be incarcerated and her healing would spring forth. My God is just amazing! He is beyond great! He cares deeply for His children. It all became so real how important the prayer watches are. Mighty works are performed when we implore heaven in alignment with each prayer watch. I'm not sure if every Christian is even aware of the prayer watches, their significance, or if they utilize the prayer watches to do damage to the kingdom of darkness. This is the basis for the million-dollar question "Are you watching?"

I've mentioned some of these scriptures before but really feel impressed to reiterate them because they are the undergirding anchors for watching and intercession:

Isaiah 59:16- He saw that there was no man, and wondered that there was no intercessor; therefore his own arm brought salvation for Him; and His own righteousness, it sustained Him.

Isaiah 62:6-7- I have set watchmen on your walls, O Jerusalem; they shall never hold their peace day or night. You who make mention of the Lord, do not keep silent, and give him no rest till He establishes and till He makes Jerusalem a praise in the earth.

Jeremiah 51:12-...make the guard strong, set up the watchmen

2 Chronicles 23:6- But let no one come into the house of the Lord except the priests, and those of the Levites who serve. They may go in for they are holy, but all the people shall keep the watch of the Lord.

We can see in the latter part of *2 Chronicles 23:6* that all Christians are encouraged to keep watch. Watching entails having clear vision, discernment, alertness, and actively monitoring all incoming and outgoing traffic. Watching also involves guarding, protecting, covering, placing a hedge around someone or something. In the old days, watchmen were strategically placed on post in elevated positions on walls of fortresses and palaces. Watchmen were expected to do just what their name mentions and that was to watch. They protected the people or city usually by pacing back and forth, visually checking every angle, and ensuring that enemies were not invading their territory. Watchmen would immediately sound the alarm and alert everyone if an enemy was intruding. This would provide an opportunity for people to seek shelter and for troops to assume both a defensive and offensive position as the enemy prepared to attack. Needless to say, the role and position of a watchmen was absolutely essential.

—

One of the key responsibilities of intercessors is to be watchmen. Intercessors require 3D vision, should oversee, and scrutinize activities transpiring in the spiritual realm. But *Matthew 26:41* admonishes us to not just watch, but watch **and** pray. Simply put, it is not enough to see, one must then sound the alarm and cry out in intercession. For your personal reference, I list the eight prayer watches at the end of this chapter. You will notice that each watch covers a three-hour time span. Many local assemblies plan their corporate and intercessory prayer times according to many of these watches. This is also one of the reasons why many churches host 24-hour prayer. Regardless of what time you visit that church, there is some room where intercessors are locked away and are praying around the clock (they utilize a rotational schedule so it is not the same individuals praying for 24 hours straight.)

Each intercessor has a specific prayer watch. Now does that mean that is the only time they should intercede? Absolutely not! The watch is when an intercessor feels most burdened to pray. For example, it does not matter how late I go to bed, without fail, I am usually up or awakened between 12 a.m. -3 a.m. (third watch of the night). Once I yield to that awakening, I am energized to pray heaven down for whatever intercessory assignment/directive the Lord gives me for that morning. There are moments when I receive intercessory burdens at different times during the day, therefore, I proceed to pray accordingly. I must say over the years, my prayer watch has remained consistent. I've heard other people mention that their watches have changed over time. It could be because the Lord is doing something new or different in you/through you. The main thing is to be aware, have revelation, and understanding of your watch.

Each watch signifies an allotted time to access certain blessings and breakthroughs. Here is a practical example for you. The bank that I use is open on Saturdays from 9:00 a.m. to 12:00 p.m. (and other times during the week). If I have specific banking needs on a Saturday that an ATM cannot address, it would be wise for me to seek entry at the time indicated by the bank. If I report to the bank at 1:00 p.m., chances are it will be closed. If a relative of yours is battling cancer, the best time to bring them before the throne via intercession is between 9:00 a.m. -12:00 a.m. Now unlike the bank scenario I gave you, it does not mean that you can't pray for them at 5:00 p.m. if you feel led. God is a gracious and merciful God. *James 5:16* lets us know that the prayer of a righteous man is powerful and effective.

The watches are merely recommended times to pray for specific things. If you know what your particular watch is, it further pinpoints the intercessory domain that God has entrusted to you. Your prayers will always be more impactful when they are aligned with heaven's schedule. If you are not familiar with the eight prayer watches, I suggest you make a copy and post it for your own reference when you are ready to intercede. Monitor when you feel most ready and burdened to pray. This will help identify your precise watch. The central/chief goal is to start watching and begin engaging in intercessory prayer.

The Eight Prayer Watches/Watching Periods
6 a.m. – 9 a.m.... The Late Morning or First Watch of the Day
- Time to command your morning
- Declarations, decrees, and utterances are released
- Time for the outpouring of the Holy Spirit- *Acts 2:4, 17, 18*

9 a.m. –12 p.m.... The Exit and Entry Watch or Second Watch of the Day

- Time for forgiveness and healing of relationships
- Time of prosperity
- Time of healing and strength
- Time for a crucified life - *Gal 2:20; Col 3:5*
- Time of inventions

12 p.m. –3 p.m.... The Watch of Shaking of Foundations & Judgment

- Promises are released
- Time to initiate change of the seven mountains such as (media)
- Time for divine guidance and deliverance from evil

3 p.m. – 6 p.m.... The Transformation Watch or Fourth Watch

- The hour of Prayer: 3:00 pm- *Acts 3:1; Acts 10:30*
- Time of covenant and removing of veils
- Time for access

6 p.m. – 9 p.m.... The Early Night Watch or First Watch of the Night

- Time for meditation
- Time for divine beginnings - *Genesis 1: 5, 8,13*
- The manifestation of the Fatherhood of God

9 p.m. – 12 a.m.... The Late Night Watch or Second Watch of the Night

- Time to Hallow and exalt the name of the Lord
- Time of prayer for ministries, religion
- Time of angelic activity and visitation

---

12 a.m. – 3 a.m....The Midnight Watch or Third Watch of the Night

- Special time for divine governments
- Time to overrule human decrees - *Exodus 12-14*
- Time for protection, strength, and increase in both Gift and Anointing

3 a.m. – 6 a.m....The Dawn or Early Morning Watch

- The Dew of the Heavens/ God releases the heavens
- Time for God's will to be done on earth as it is willed in heaven
- Time of heavy visitation

Chapter Eight:

"COVER ME AS I COVER YOU"

From the previous chapters, we can truly see the importance and power behind intercession. Heaven has yet to reveal all the breakthroughs received because of faithful intercessors who did not abandon their posts. Selfless is the mindset and heart of the intercessor who will stop, drop, and pray when heaven beckons. Sacrificing their time, energy, schedule and sleep. Your senior pastor has been interceding for you, your mentor has been interceding for you, and your ministry colleague has been bombarding heaven on your behalf. Oh how we thank God for them! But did you ever wonder, who covers the intercessor?

The reality is that ministry can be physically, emotionally, and spiritually grueling. I think of the tears intercessors shed on behalf of others. The pacing back and forth from room to room, as if to stomp the enemy harder with every step they take. Lying prostrate for hours on their faces, bending over until ashy knees have become their permanent reward, or the intense travail with an inward pleading of mercy for the birth to come sooner than later. This can only be described as faith and love in action!

Please, as they cover you, don't forget to throw a warm, plush blanket over them as well. The gates of hell are relentless in attacking the soldiers enlisted in the Lord's army (especially those positioned on the front lines). Make no mistake about it! Every intercessor needs an intercessor. The devil could care less about the souls he already has in his clutches. He laughs at individuals that are spiritually asleep and encourages them to pop more sleeping pills.

The watchmen are a different breed altogether. Satan gnashes his teeth at the intercessors who are wide awake, conserving the family gate, monitoring the gate of education, guarding the gate of government, standing watch at the gate of business and finance, preserving the gate of religion, defending the gate of arts and entertainment and surveying the gate of media and technology.

Yes, intercessors are among the enemy's greatest threats. Every great soldier becomes weary at some point. Therefore, intercessors need Aarons and Hurs that will lift up their arms, as they undergird the arms of others. After they've battled demonic principalities and powers, intercessors must be insulated from the backlashes of hell. This will empower them to keep standing, remain persistent in watching, and to continue fighting. It is not uncommon for intercessors to win many wars for others, they sometimes have not won for themselves. While they stand in the trenches for you, they pay a dear price in one or more areas of their personal lives.

Their finances, marriages, children, health, minds, businesses, and/or ministries, experience heavy assault. Remember, intercessors stand watch at the gates. They sound the alarm and cry out to warn others of impending danger, but they cannot leave their post. When the enemy attacks any gate, intercessors take quite a few hits. The weight of the constant beating and pounding can cause anyone at any time to buckle under the pressure. Without the proper spiritual covering, backing, and protection, intercessors can become susceptible and vulnerable to fatigue, sickness, depression, discouragement, despair, feelings of loneliness, isolation, apathy, and much more.

In *Mark 2:1-12* we read a story of four men who carry a paralytic, and do the unthinkable by tearing a hole in the roof, pressing their way through the crowd, to lower their friend to Jesus for healing. I would like to take the liberty to briefly eisegete from this text rather than exegete. Looking through prophetic lenses, the four men may have been the prophet, evangelist, pastor, and teacher that was carrying the apostle. Or they may have been the apostle, prophet, pastor, and teacher, undergirding the evangelist. Or perhaps, it was the apostle, prophet, evangelist, and teacher that was lifting up the pastor.

They were holding up one of the Gifts given to the Body of Christ. These men clearly understood that it would be of no benefit to the church and to the world if one of their soldiers were wounded, not on his post/not fulfilling his assignment. They said "Devil you are a liar and still a deceiver. Not on my watch will any Gift or intercessor remain down." They rebuked the spirit of Cain in Genesis Chapter 4 who cynically said to God "Am I my brother's Keeper?" God answered him in Ephesians 4 saying Yes, you are your brother's keeper, you are called to build, edify, and hold up one another. The bed that these men carried the paralytic on was the bed of Intercession. They brought him to Jesus, the one who was able to heal and revive.

You see, in order to travel from one mountain peak to another (which represents moments of victory), one has to descend back into the valley (low place). Every Christian can attest to the fact that low places in our lives are very real. Thanks be to God that greater is He that is in us, than he that is in the world *(1 John 4:4)*. *And those who wait upon the Lord shall renew their strength (Isaiah 40:31)*. However, while intercessors maneuver through the valley, we have to intercede for them so they don't make their permanent residence there (Defensive Intercession).

We must also stand in the gap for them when they are on the mountain top so they can withstand the heat in the valley (Preventative Intercession).

Just as police officers wear bullet proof vests, intercessors must put spiritual safeguards in place to ensure that they are not overwhelmed and overtaken by the enemy. *Ephesians 6:13-18* reminds us to put on the full armor of God. You may refer back to chapter five for other means of protection. Another important safeguard is to surround yourself with trusted, loyal, and dependable individuals you know will intercede for you.

I know for a fact my Senior Pastors intercede for me, our congregation, our city, and our nation. Senior Pastors are the true intercessory MVPs for the Body of Christ. The ministerial burdens and weights they carry are tremendous. It is our responsibility to intercede for them daily. We should do our very best not to add an unnecessary load to their existing spiritual cargo. We drain our pastors when we do so. As much as we'd like for them to be, they cannot be all things to all men. So, intercessor, get yourself some intercessors! I have been blessed with a very small, inner circle, who undergirds me via intercession. We each enjoy having our own space and breathing room. Each of us are "doing our own thang". We understand when it's time to assemble and discern when we just need to be alone with our God. Yet when one sounds the alarm, you better believe we come running.

There are occasions I am experiencing attacks that I am unable to verbalize or am too tired to reach out. Their spiritual radar will pick me up. They will call and say "What's going on with you? I'm sensing this." We send each other prayer alerts/requests. In many instances, when wisdom dictates, we don't interfere (we don't say), we just pray. We get together every so often to do personal and spiritual briefings about finances, children, our jobs, our callings, anointings, projects, short term, and long term goals etc. We spend time discussing God's Word and interceding for each other. Words of wisdom are exchanged. They hold me accountable and I do the same for them. We tell each other the truth in LOVE and we keep it moving. No offense taken. I can let my hair down, cry, laugh, vent, and just be myself around these precious gifts. When we are at spiritual gatherings, they honor me by calling me Prophetess Joanne, and likewise, I honor the title/office God has called them to. We are never clingy, so you would never be able to tell just how tight we are. When it's just us hanging out, they call me by my nickname Jojo or Jo, and I love it!

I am single, a mother of two teenage children, a full time teacher, a student, a sister, a daughter, and heavily involved in ministry. If I didn't have my spiritual Peter, James, and John who cover me in intercession, Lord only knows where I'd be right now! You need individuals like this in your life. People who are not enamored by your gift, or impressed by the fact that you are Prophet Eagle Red Eye, Chief Bishop of the Honorary Holy Ghost Board, or The Apostle over the Shining Apostles (you'd be surprised the crazy titles people assign themselves). We are clear that no one will ever or can ever take the place of God. He comes before everyone and everything. Yet, one of the significant ways the Lord expresses His love and Himself is through covenant/divine relationships, which are a valuable asset/commodity in the Kingdom of God.

My advice to each intercessor is DO NOT do ministry alone! DO NOT do intercession alone! Now, to the Body of Christ, I charge you to fervently and continually pray for our intercessors. Their silent heart's cry is "Cover me as I cover you!"

Chapter Nine:

PROPHETIC INTERCESSION

*" **But** if they are **prophets** and if the word of the Lord is with them, let them now make **intercession** to the Lord of hosts, that the vessels which are left in the house of the Lord, in the house of the king of Judah, and at Jerusalem, do not go to Babylon."*
-Jeremiah 27:18

I love the above scripture because it is self- explanatory. The prophetic is married to intercession. Not all intercessors are prophets, but all prophets bear the responsibility of intercession. I am called to the office of the prophet *(Ephesians 4:11)* and was publically affirmed by my senior leaders. Therefore, I engage in prophetic intercession on a regular basis. Not all, but some of the information I am about to disclose may overlap with details I've shared in earlier chapters. That is quite alright. Just think of it as a second helping of your favorite dessert. I will briefly mention the six branches of prayer that is listed in my spiritual father, Apostle Bryan Meadows' book *Prophetic Science*. My objective here is to park and delve into prophetic intercession (interchangeable with prophetic prayers) for those who are prophets and feel they are called to that office.

6 Branches of Prayer

1. **Thanksgiving and Praise-** Expressing gratitude and just loving on the Lord/Shabaching Him/adoring Him.
- *Psalm 100:4- Enter into His gates with Thanksgiving and into His courts with praise.*
- *Psalm 34:1- I will bless the Lord at all times; His raise shall continually be in my mouth.*
- *Psalm 107:1- Oh give thanks to the Lord, for He is good!*

2. <u>**Petition and Supplication**</u>- Making request/asking for yourself but mostly on behalf of others, this is usually your grocery list of prayers.

- *__Ephesians 6:18__- Praying always with all prayer and supplication in the Spirit.*
- *__Philippians 4:6__- Be anxious for nothing, but in everything by prayer and supplication, with thanksgiving, let your requests be made known to God.*
- *__I John 5:15__- And if we know that He hears us, whatever we ask, we know we have the petitions that we have asked of Him.*
- *__Psalm 20:5__... May the Lord fulfill all your petitions.*

3. <u>**Proclamations and Decrees**</u>- You releasing a command or giving an order in prayer. You are essentially passing law via your prayers. This is done of course from a place of Christ's authority. *__Ephesians 1:3__* says that *God has blessed us with every spiritual blessing in the heavenly places in Christ Jesus.* This is not your asking or begging type of prayers. You are telling that thing where to go and how to do it.

- *__Job 22:28__- You will also declare a thing and it will be established for you...*
- *__Psalm 2:7__- I will declare the decree the Lord ; the Lord said to me, You are my Son, today I have begotten You.*
- *__Psalm 148:6__- He also established them forever; He made a decree which shall not pass away.*

4. <u>**Tongues and Mysteries (Groaning and Weeping)**</u>- Deep cry and travail by the spirit within when words are simply inadequate.

- *Romans 8:26-* *Likewise the Spirit also helps in our weaknesses. For we do not know what we should pray for as we ought, but the Spirit Himself makes intercession for us with groanings which cannot be uttered.*
- *John 11:33-* *Jesus groaned in the Spirit and was troubled at the news of Lazarus' death and in* *Matthew 26:37* *in the Garden of Gethsemane.*
- *Psalm 6:6-* *I am weary of my groaning; all night I make my bed swim; I drench my couch with my tears.*
- *Romans 8:22-* *For we know that the whole creation groans and labors with birth pangs together until now.*

5. **Apostolic Blessing and Impartation-** Which comes by way of a Spiritual Father/Covering *Hebrews 11:21* - Jacob leaning on his staff (rank) to bless his children. This is the blessing of sonship.

6. **Prophetic Intercession-** **Prophetic Intercession is NOT:**

- Habitual/repetitious- Examples: "Now I lay me down to sleep..." or "Hail Mary full of Grace the Lord is with thee."
- Copying the exact way someone else prays.
- There are laws that govern the spiritual world and if you don't understand those laws, you can bring serious harm to yourself. These individuals operate in a certain grace and anointing which may be different from your grace and anointing. So you have to stay in your lane and move at your own speed.

Allow God to use your own personality, voice, and expression. You don't want to pray other people's prayers verbatim but never get what is for you.

- You may say Prophetess Joanne isn't the first level of impartation modeling and imitating? Didn't Paul say follow me as I follow Christ? Yes, that is true. But you have to know who to follow and understand the spiritual dynamics behind everything that you do.
- It is not utilizing prayer for your own selfish reasons or to inflict harm on someone (Example: Lord you see the pain they caused me. I prophesy worse will be done to them). These kind of prayers will keep the heavens shut over your head.

What Prophetic Intercession is:

- There were 3 main offices in the Old Testament that were anointed. The Office of the King, Priest, and the Prophet. The King had rulership and exercised the authority to legislate. The Priest's job was to go to God on behalf of man. The Prophet always went to man on behalf of God. Prophetic Praying is a merging of these two functions and responsibilities. When you get into decreeing/declaring, you are actually converging all three functions.

- Prophetic Intercession involves prophesying while praying.

- Prophetic Intercession goes beyond just saying prayers and talking with the Lord. It is prayer that is inspired by the breath and the Holy Spirit of the living God/God breathed or the wind of God. The Hebrew word for that is **Ruach** which is similar to the Greek word **Pneuma**.

Remember Jesus says His words are spirit and life. The question I have for you is: When was the last time you prayed something that totally surprised you or that you were not expecting?

- Prophetic Prayers pull God's will into the earth realm. We truly need deposits (whether it be deposits of power, wisdom, strength, revelation etc.) from heaven in order to effectively impact the natural realm. That's why according to **Matthew 6:10** we pray *"Your Kingdom come, your will be done on earth as it is in heaven."*

- For us to maneuver further into the deep things of God and to access all the hidden treasures God has for our lives, family, finances, our ministries, our cities, our nation etc. We need revelation and power more than ever. One of the keys to unlocking that revelation and power is prophetic prayers. It is a realm of intercession that goes beyond human capacity and taps into the supernatural. Scripture says that the weapons of our warfare are not carnal, but are mighty through God to the pulling down of strongholds.

- Prophetic People/Prophets have the ability through their prayers to go into the future to fight and lay hold of all that God wants to manifest in their lives.

- Paul once said to Timothy that he must fight concerning the prophecies spoken over him. Often times we think just because a prophetic word has been released, it will automatically happen. Strategic Intercession and warfare are often needed to guard and to activate pressure in the spirit realm for these prophecies to manifest in the natural/earth realm.

- We must understand that unlike you and me the enemy never goes on vacation. Like a thief he is always seeking an opportunity to kill, steal, and destroy. Therefore, it is the responsibility of engaging in prophetic prayers that will arrest the spirits of Cain, Pharaoh, Saul, and Herod. Cain will kill you out of anger, rage, and jealousy. Pharaoh will attack during a time of birthing and emergence. Saul attacks during seasons of promotion and elevation. Herod will seek to assassinate your destiny and purpose.

- Prophetic Intercession reveals your enemies, their schemes, plans, where they are, and what they are doing.

- We can't be timid. **Matthew 11:12** says *"And from the days of John the Baptist until now, the kingdom of heaven suffers violence and the violent take it by force."* We do so not in our own strength but by prophetic prayers.

To be activated in Prophetic Intercession:
1. **You must be a born-again believer.**

2. **You have to be trained in prayer.** That is why the disciples asked Jesus to teach them how to pray (workshops/training centers/prayer conferences/s).

3. **Be filled with the Holy Ghost with the evidence of speaking in tongues.** The spiritual realm is a world unto itself. The prophetic is also a world unto itself. Each

———
110

world has its own culture, language and customs. In the spiritual and prophetic world, tongues is like your passport that will gain you access into that world. It is your heavenly language. If you go to a foreign country, you cannot effectively interact or make exchanges without speaking that language.

4. **Be in the presence of God-** *Psalm 91- He who dwells in the secret place of the Most High.* If you are going to pray prayers that are God breathed, you have to get close enough *(John 20:22-And when He said this, He breathed on them and said to them "Receive the Holy Spirit.")* The secret chamber is also where God trains you to hear His voice.

5. **God must trust you.** People will only share secrets with those they trust. Can you be trusted or will you run and disclose everything the Lord reveals to you? *Amos 3:7 Surely the Lord God does nothing unless He reveals His secret to His servants the Prophets/Prophetic People.*

6. **Remain sensitive-** Often you will receive a word of wisdom or word of knowledge, phrase, a burden will drop down, a face will come before you, a name, a song, a vision, an image/or picture (Examples: someone twirling and their clothing falling off may signify freedom. Someone climbing a mountain may represent journey, sacrifice, elevation etc.)

7. **Once you receive a word, you engage in prophetic intercession to birth it out.**

In Summary

1. Prophetic Intercession produces pressure and unleashes the supernatural power of God.
2. There are so many prophecies that hang over our heads unfulfilled because we don't pray prophetically. Prophetic Intercession give legs to prophetic words and causes those words to run to the finish line.
3. Strategic Intercession unlocks specific answers.
4. How we pray is just as (if not more) significant as what we pray.
5. Prophetic Intercession in the life of the Church and in the lives of believers must be activated, evident, consistent, and on-going.

At this time, I would like to release a prophetic word that I shared back in 2011 with a group of intercessors. I strongly believe this word is more alive and applicable today than it ever was.

Wildfire (Sunday, February 2, 2011)
For over a month now, I've been having visions of fire. The fire I keep seeing is out of control and it is ablaze. I see **tongues of fire** descending upon the **head of each Intercessor** and then on the heads of every member of the Body of Christ. The Lord says that He is moving like **wildfire** (that was the exact word) and He is going to consume **everything**. We must keep in mind though, that fire has different functions:

Fire burns- Fire burns away all impurities. Everything that is in us that is not of God has got to go. All our idols, crutches, distractions, and sins will be consumed by the fire. God will consume it all. We can yield the easy way or He will consume it the hard way.

This is God as a wildfire: *Hebrews 12:28, 29- Therefore, since we are receiving a kingdom which cannot be shaken, let us have grace, by which we may serve God acceptably with reverence and godly fear. For our God is a consuming fire.*

<u>Fire rages</u>- Wildfires are often out of control, they spread quickly, and they are hard to contain. The Lord says that once sin is dealt with, we are going to experience the following: **Wildfire Anointing, Wildfire Hunger for the Lord, Wildfire Cleansing, Wildfire Love, Wildfire Peace, Wildfire Provision, Wildfire Ministries, Wildfire Worship, Wildfire Praise, Wildfire Devotion, Wildfire Boldness, and Wildfire Prayers. This is us experiencing the wildfire (see Acts Chapter 2).**

In regards to Wildfire Devotion, the Lord wants **single devotion**. We can no longer sit for endless hours in front of the T.V., in front of Facebook, on our phones and give God bare minimum. God wants us to be different from the world. He is not going to compete with any distractions. God is looking for single devotion to Him. *Colossians 3:1, 2- If then you were raised with Christ, seek those things which are above, where Christ is sitting at the right hand of God. Set your mind on things above, and not on things on the earth.*

<u>Fire ignites, gives light, and gives heat</u>- God is coming to set us **ablaze**. We are going to be like a match or torch that cannot be put out (literally). When the fire is ablaze in us, **everything and everyone** that comes around us will catch on fire too. It will be contagious and out of control. You won't be able to contain the fire of God's Holy Spirit. We will give off light (for we are the light of the world), and we will give off heat to those around.

The backslider and those that are not saved will experience the heat, warmth, and light of the fire that we give off and they will get right with the Lord. The fire is also representative of the **Anointing**. God is looking for clean vessels to use. He cannot anoint impure vessels. He wants us to be vessels of glory and honor for Him. **It is not about us. God has work for us to do. It is about His will being done.** There are prayers to be prayed and souls to intercede for. God says it is time for each Intercessor to arise and step up. We cannot sit back any longer. We look at others and think they are the anointed ones who are supposed to do all the praying and we sit back and watch. We cannot allow just the two or three people to uphold the prayer burdens. You are just as important as anyone else. **The anointing is for each and every one of us.** We are called to intercessory ministry. Some of us are supposed to stand in the gap but we don't. No longer is this acceptable. It is time to arise. The fire will and must start with us as intercessors before it runs rampant to the rest of the Body of Christ. **This is us as a wildfire (see *Jeremiah 20:9*, and the rest of the book of Acts). You are a wildfire intercessor!**

<u>**Now recite this prayer**</u>- *Lord purify me with your refiner's fire. If there be anything in me that is unlike you, please burn it away. Today and forever, I submit to your Lordship. Mold me, shape me, fashion me, and cleanse me until you see a reflection of your Son Jesus in my life. Lord I know you have called me to be a co-laborer with Christ but I refuse to speak, move, or do anything apart from the anointing and fire of your Holy Spirit. Set me ablaze Lord that I might be a vessel of glory and honor for you to use. Let my life give off heat and light to a dying world that they too may come to know you as Savior. I decree and declare that I am a wildfire intercessor. I will pray, speak, and minister when you ask me to. Let me experience the tongues of fire that you promised (in me, through me, and towards me). I receive it by faith. In Jesus name I pray. Amen!*

Chapter Ten:

INTERCESSORY REFLECTIONS

$\mathcal{T}$hrough this book, I was able to share several of my personal experiences and discussed how each situation drove me to a deeper place in intercession. Beyond that, I trust you were able to glean helpful truths pertaining to intercession, and were encouraged to embrace your own divine interruptions (with an understanding of the WHY behind each situation). Remember, it is the responsibility of every believer to intercede/keep watch *(2 Chronicles 23:6)*. It is my earnest prayer that your intercessory womb would begin to expand and contract to release God's will and agenda here on earth. For this final chapter, I would like for you to take a moment or a couple of days to reflect and record your own mental processing and understanding of the information I released in *Interrupted to Intercede*. I lay out specific questions on each page to guide you in accomplishing this task.

List 7 truths you already knew about intercession:

List 8 or more revelatory nuggets that you learned from this book:_____

_____

_____

_____

_____

_____

_____

_____

_____

_____

_____

_____

_____

_____

_____

_____

_____

_____

_____

_____

_____

_____

_____

_____

_____

_____

_____

_____

_____

_____

_____

_____

_____

_____

_____

Have you ever engaged in intercessory prayer/prophetic prayer? If yes, when did you first become aware that you were called to be an intercessor?

Briefly describe any intercessory training you have received. If you have not received any training, what actions will you take to be trained (example: join Intercessory team at church, get an intercessory mentor etc.)?

From your own personal experience, what has been some of the most rewarding aspects of intercession?

What are some challenges you've discovered as it pertains to intercession?

Share a dream or vision you've had that immediately drove you to intercede on behalf of a person, place, or event.

Be honest with yourself. Have you dealt with your past hurt, pain, and disappointments in order to become an effective intercessor? If your answer is yes, briefly describe your journey in getting to freedom. If your answer is no, what strategy or plan mentioned in chapter five will you implement/pursue to ensure your ticket to wholeness?

Do you know what your prayer watch is? If yes, how do you know?

_____
_____
_____
_____
_____
_____
_____
_____
_____
_____
_____
_____
_____
_____
_____
_____
_____
_____
_____
_____
_____
_____
_____
_____
_____
_____
_____
_____
_____
_____
_____
_____

Who are your personal intercessors/midwives? How have they impacted your life?

List the individuals you intercede for on a consistent basis. Give one specific example of a life that has been changed by your intercessory prayers.

Identify an Intercessor in the Bible that stands out to you. Tell us the WHO, WHAT, WHEN, WHERE, and WHY behind their intercession. Please be sure to jot down the scripture reference(s).

What changes/improvements will you make as you proceed in your intercessory journey? (Example: more time reading the Word of God, fasting once per week, addressing past hurts etc.)

Based on the changes/improvements you jotted down, write a prayer to the Lord. Then spend 15 minutes engaging in prayer for your request.

_____

_____

_____

_____

_____

_____

_____

_____

_____

_____

_____

_____

_____

_____

_____

_____

_____

_____

_____

_____

_____

_____

_____

_____

_____

_____

_____

_____

_____

_____

_____

Share your final thoughts on *Interrupted to Intercede*:

Made in the USA
Columbia, SC
02 February 2025

53104308R00074